Ready, Set, Edit:
Over 170 Daily Editing Mini-Lessons

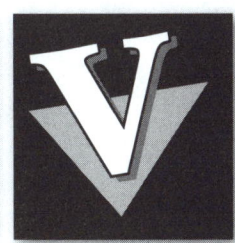

Connie Prevatte

Rigby Best Teachers Press
An imprint of Rigby

Dedication
To Sam…and other children beginning their journey into the world of writing

Editors: Julia Moses and Mary Susnis
Executive Editor: Georgine Cooper
Designer: Nancy Rudd
Design Production Manager: Tom Sjoerdsma
Cover Illustrator: Terry Sirrell

ISBN 0-7578-2102-2

© 2002 Harcourt Achieve Inc.
All rights reserved. Pages 7–186 of this book are intended for classroom use and not for resale or distribution. These pages may be reproduced, with the copyright notice, without permission from the Publisher. Reproduction for an entire school or district is prohibited. No other part of this publication may be reproduced or transmitted in any form or by any means, electronic or mechanical, including photocopying, recording, taping, or any information storage and retrieval system, without permission in writing from the Publisher. Contact: Copyright Permissions, Harcourt Achieve Inc., P.O. Box 27010, Austin, TX 78755.

Rigby and Steck-Vaughn are trademarks of Harcourt Achieve Inc. registered in the United States of America and/or other jurisdictions.

08 07
10 9 8 7 6 5 4

Printed in the United States of America.

Writing Class Format

Students need writing instruction daily. A 40-45 minute writing class consists of four distinct components:

Editing Mini-Lesson	3 to 5 minutes
Revision Mini-Lesson	4 to 8 minutes
Writing Process	2 to 28 minutes
Sharing	5 minutes

How to Use This Book

Editing Mini-Lessons are used as a tool to teach correct grammatical usage, effective use of punctuation, recognition of spelling errors, and appropriate use of capitalization. The instructional focus of the daily Editing Mini-Lesson is determined by the needs of the students. If you observe many students having difficulty identifying misspelled words, a spelling mini-lesson may be presented and taught.

To provide direct instruction, create transparencies from the following pages. Then place the lesson transparency on the overhead projector and elicit responses from students about the errors, corrections, and rules. A brisk pace is important. If a lesson moves too slowly, students' attention may wander. Make corrections directly on the transparency or on a blank transparency placed over the lesson. Students should not copy the transparency. Instead, they should engage themselves in reading the text and searching for errors.

GIFTED EDUCATION
Orange County Schools

The Ten-Day Cycle of Mini-Lessons

DAY ONE	**Sentence Category**
DAY TWO	**Sentence Category**
DAY THREE	**Sentence Category**
DAY FOUR	**Sentence Category**
DAY FIVE	**Paragraph**
DAY SIX	**Sentence Category**
DAY SEVEN	**Sentence Category**
DAY EIGHT	**Sentence Category**
DAY NINE	**Sentence Category**
DAY TEN	**Test (Assessment)**

The category of the Editing Mini-Lesson used each day is determined by student need. The sentence categories are: usage, punctuation, capitalization, spelling, variety, and paragraphs.

An Editing Mini-Lesson using paragraph format should be used on a consistent basis. Certain editing skills can only be taught in paragraph format.

The assessments do not use new text. It is reproduced from one of the previous lessons in the cycle. Do not have students copy the text from the transparency. Instead, reproduce the lesson and distribute it to each student. Because you are using one of the lessons already covered, you are not only assessing student proficiency, but also providing students a reason to be engaged during all lessons.

Contents

Usage Lessons 1–30 — **7–36**

Punctuation Lessons 1–30 — **37–66**

Capitalization Lessons 1–30 — **67–96**

Spelling Lessons 1–30 — **97–126**

Variety Lessons 1–30 — **127–156**

Paragraphs Lessons 1–30 — **157–186**

Answer Key — **187–200**

Usage / Lesson 1

Juan and me is going to the movies.

The children, screaming loudly, wents out to play.

<u>Tom</u> and Sue <u>are</u> playing
 A   B

with Joyce and <u>I</u>. (<u>none</u>)
                C   D

☐ A   ☐ B   ☐ C   ☐ D

Usage / Lesson 2

Devin run every morning in the fall.

Greg and Meagan been in two plays.

David taught Bill and me
 A   B
all he know about math.
        C
(none)
  D

☐ A   ☐ B   ☐ C   ☐ D

Usage / Lesson 3

Each student should complete their test.

Everyone jumped on their bike.

<u>Neither</u> of the boys
  A

<u>brought</u> <u>his books</u> to class.
   B   C

(<u>none</u>)
  D

☐ A   ☐ B   ☐ C   ☐ D

Usage / Lesson 4

The teacher blamed we girls for everything.

Kyle is shorter than me.

My teacher took Janet and I to the game. (none)
  A   B   C   D

☐ A ☐ B ☐ C ☐ D

Usage / Lesson 5

Each student should open their book.

Neither of the girls could not find her ball.

Many of the students wore his uniforms. (none)
  A   B   C   D

☐ A   ☐ B   ☐ C   ☐ D

Usage / Lesson 6

The children drunk their juice.

It was the warmer day of the year.

Both of them ran well, but Carl was the fastest. (none)
A   B   C   D

☐ A ☐ B ☐ C ☐ D

Usage / Lesson 7

A group of sixth graders have been playing here.

A herd of cows were sighted near the road.

<u>Neither</u> the book <u>or</u> the paper <u>was</u> clean. (<u>none</u>)
  A   B   C   D

❏ A   ❏ B   ❏ C   ❏ D

Usage / Lesson 8

In this story, the spelling and grammar is poor.

In the school, there is three sixth grade classes.

Neither the car <u>nor</u> the
⠀⠀⠀⠀⠀⠀⠀⠀⠀⠀⠀⠀A

truck <u>is</u> <u>broken</u>. (<u>none</u>)
⠀⠀⠀⠀B⠀⠀C⠀⠀⠀⠀⠀⠀D

❏ A ❏ B ❏ C ❏ D

Usage / Lesson 9

Ninety percent of the class are sick.

Matthew thought the guilty person was me.

Tom and <u>she</u> thought it
       A

<u>was</u> <u>me</u>.   (<u>none</u>)
 B   C   D

☐ A   ☐ B   ☐ C   ☐ D

Usage / Lesson 10

There is several reasons for checking his scores.

Everyone expected they to win the game.

The teacher <u>asked</u> <u>us</u> girls
      A   B

<u>to correct</u> the papers.
    C

(<u>none</u>)
   D

☐ A ☐ B ☐ C ☐ D

Usage / Lesson 11

They are smarter than us.

If we was rich, we would purchase a new computer.

<u>May</u> <u>us</u> girls use the computers <u>?</u>   (<u>none</u>)
 A   B   C   D

☐ A   ☐ B   ☐ C   ☐ D

Usage / Lesson 12

I can not clean the table.

The new teacher don't like teaching her science class.

<u>The</u> team <u>is</u> <u>already</u> for
 A   B   C
the game. (<u>none</u>)
                D

☐ A   ☐ B   ☐ C   ☐ D

Usage / Lesson 13

Paul is all ready late for class.

We can not attend the rock concert.

Jim <u>sure</u> <u>is</u> <u>smart</u>.
　　A　B　　C

(<u>none</u>)
　D

☐ A　☐ B　☐ C　☐ D

Usage / Lesson 14

I didn't have no time to do my homework.

Joshua was laying on the sofa.

Last night I lay in bed to watch TV. (none)
 A   B   C   D

☐ A ☐ B ☐ C ☐ D

Usage / Lesson 15

He sat his book on the desk.

The Thanksgiving dinner tasted extra good.

Frank was sitting at his desk. (none)
 A   B   C   D

☐ A   ☐ B   ☐ C   ☐ D

Usage / Lesson 16

Moira is fixin the broken table.

A carton of eggs are on the table.

Jake, as well as his five friends, are tired of the game. (none)
  A   B   C   D

☐ A   ☐ B   ☐ C   ☐ D

Usage / Lesson 17

The boys is always arguing among themselves.

The class are winning the contest.

Hamburger and fries is my favorite lunch. (none)
A   B   C   D

☐ A   ☐ B   ☐ C   ☐ D

Usage / Lesson 18

Either James or Kelly are to wash the dishes.

Paulo's sister received a A on the test.

$\underline{\text{The}}$ football team $\underline{\text{it wins}}$
 A   B
the games$\underline{.}$ ($\underline{\text{none}}$)
         C   D

☐ A   ☐ B   ☐ C   ☐ D

Usage / Lesson 19

The suds is spilling on the floor.

Nobody in the class have finished the test.

Her clothes are very stylish. (none)
 A   B
 C   D

☐ A   ☐ B   ☐ C   ☐ D

Usage / Lesson 20

Every student brought their book.

The dog has it's bone.

As the class <u>entered</u> the
         A
room, the teacher <u>looked</u>
                    B
at <u>their</u> faces. (<u>none</u>)
     C   D

☐ A ☐ B ☐ C ☐ D

Usage / Lesson 21

It was her who painted the picture.

If I were him, I would scream.

The game <u>was</u> exciting <u>to</u>
         A   B
Daniel and <u>he</u>. (<u>none</u>)
           C   D

☐ A ☐ B ☐ C ☐ D

Usage / Lesson 22

The teacher liked everyone but David and I.

When Alex seen the dog running down the street, he begin to tremble.

When I came home from school, she will be cooking dinner. (none)
   A   B   C   D

☐ A   ☐ B   ☐ C   ☐ D

Usage / Lesson 23

Did David brung the book back yet?

Nick did, I am sure, ran to his class.

Kara and I doesn't know the answer. (none)
　　　　　A　　B　　　C　　　　　　　D

☐ A　☐ B　☐ C　☐ D

Usage / Lesson 24

Jake decided to walk slow and easy toward the house.

They played good in the tournament.

She and <u>I</u> <u>wrote</u> a <u>real</u>
　　　　A　　　B　　　　C

good essay. (<u>none</u>)
　　　　　　　　D

☐ A　☐ B　☐ C　☐ D

Usage / Lesson 25

We was late due to a power outage.

We practices for the play in the auditorium.

<u>He is</u> in trouble <u>cause</u> he
 A   B

<u>broke</u> the rules. (<u>none</u>)
 C   D

☐ A   ☐ B   ☐ C   ☐ D

Usage / Lesson 26

Where is the book at?

Her face, sweaty and pale, were full of fear.

Chuck and I didn't hardly touch our lunch. (none)
　　　　　A　　　　　B　　　　　　C　　　　　D

☐ A ☐ B ☐ C ☐ D

Usage / Lesson 27

Tony fell off of his bike.

Jackie blame Greg for the fight.

Zack and I got out of the car quickly. (none)
　　　　A　　　B　　　　　C　　　D

☐ A　☐ B　☐ C　☐ D

Usage / Lesson 28

She was angry at his dad.

I doesn't know if I passed the test.

It <u>looks</u> like <u>it's</u> going to <u>snow</u>. (<u>none</u>)
    A   B   C   D

☐ A   ☐ B   ☐ C   ☐ D

Usage / Lesson 29

Read that poem to John and I.

The skiers, Mary and her, plunged down the hill.

Mrs. Jones <u>didn't</u> like <u>my</u> asking so many <u>questions</u>.
             A   B   C
(<u>none</u>)
  D

☐ A   ☐ B   ☐ C   ☐ D

Usage / Lesson 30

The door's lock were broken.

He don't know the answer.

Tammy <u>worked</u> <u>quick</u> in
       A   B
order to finish <u>her</u>
                 C
homework. (<u>none</u>)
            D

☐ A ☐ B ☐ C ☐ D

Punctuation / Lesson 1

Michael his father is going to work

He loaded his plate with chicken fish and bread

Carol said, "Where is the
         A
pie, Kelly"? (none)
 B   C   D

☐ A   ☐ B   ☐ C   ☐ D

Punctuation / Lesson 2

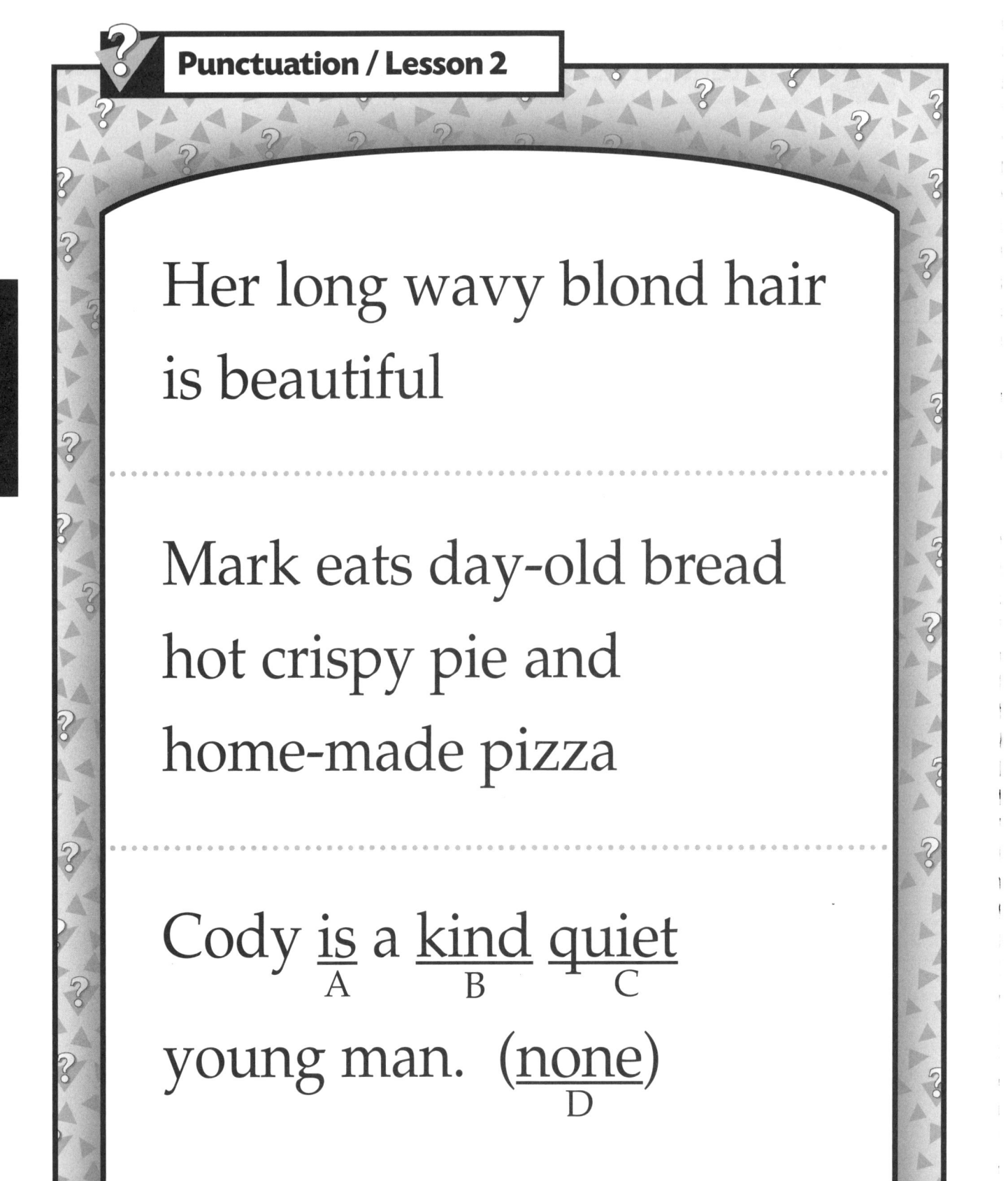

Her long wavy blond hair is beautiful

Mark eats day-old bread hot crispy pie and home-made pizza

Cody is a kind quiet young man. (none)
     A   B   C   D

☐ A   ☐ B   ☐ C   ☐ D

Punctuation / Lesson 3

Joe wants to play ball but, I want to read

George wants to play ball and, read

Ron woke <u>up,</u> and <u>tried</u> to
           A   B
fall back to <u>sleep.</u> (<u>none</u>)
              C   D

☐ A   ☐ B   ☐ C   ☐ D

Punctuation / Lesson 4

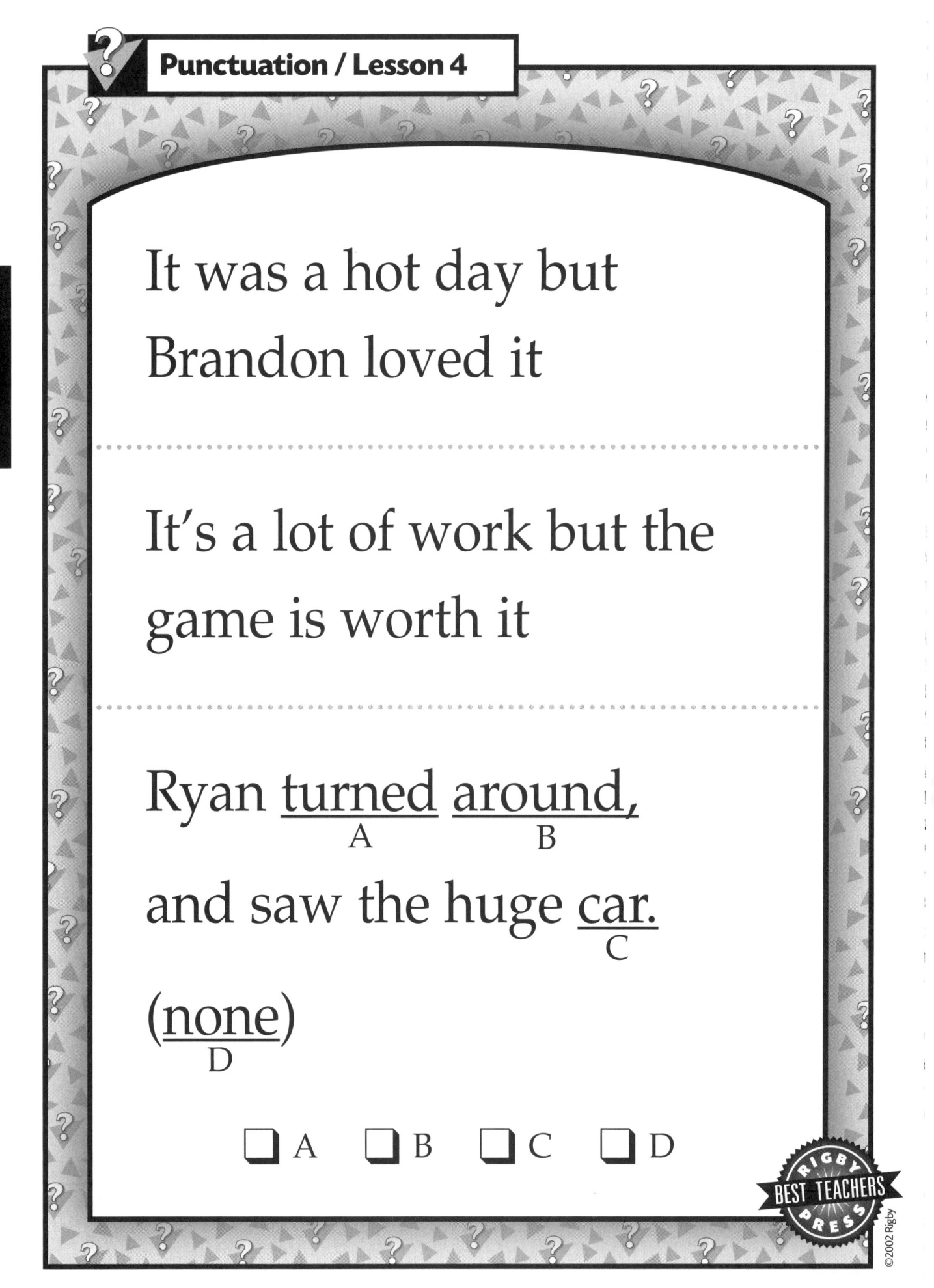

It was a hot day but Brandon loved it

It's a lot of work but the game is worth it

Ryan <u>turned</u> <u>around,</u> and saw the huge <u>car.</u>
     A   B   C

(<u>none</u>)
  D

☐ A   ☐ B   ☐ C   ☐ D

Punctuation / Lesson 5

Because I want a good grade I will study hard

I will study hard because I want a good grade

<u>At</u> the edge of the <u>pool</u> he
 A   B

<u>relaxed</u> in the sun. (<u>none</u>)
   C   D

☐ A   ☐ B   ☐ C   ☐ D

Punctuation / Lesson 6

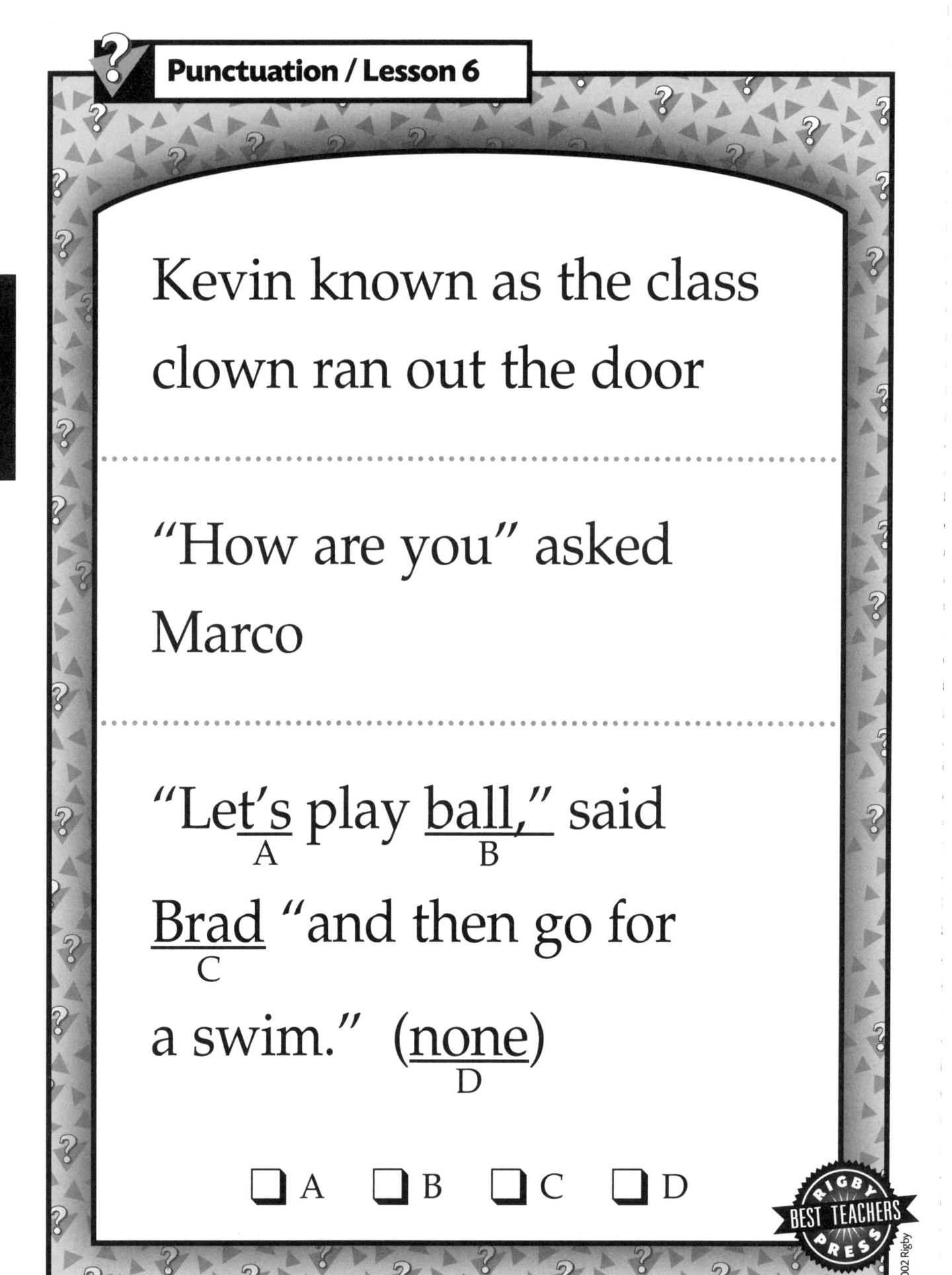

Kevin known as the class clown ran out the door

"How are you" asked Marco

"Le<u>t's</u> play <u>ball,</u>" said
   A   B

<u>Brad</u> "and then go for
  C

a swim." (<u>none</u>)
              D

☐ A ☐ B ☐ C ☐ D

Punctuation / Lesson 7

No I do not want another book

Sam I think is a wonderful student

Mr. <u>Lamb,</u> the oldest man in <u>town</u> will speak to the <u>class.</u> (<u>none</u>)
     A   B   C   D

☐ A   ☐ B   ☐ C   ☐ D

Punctuation / Lesson 8

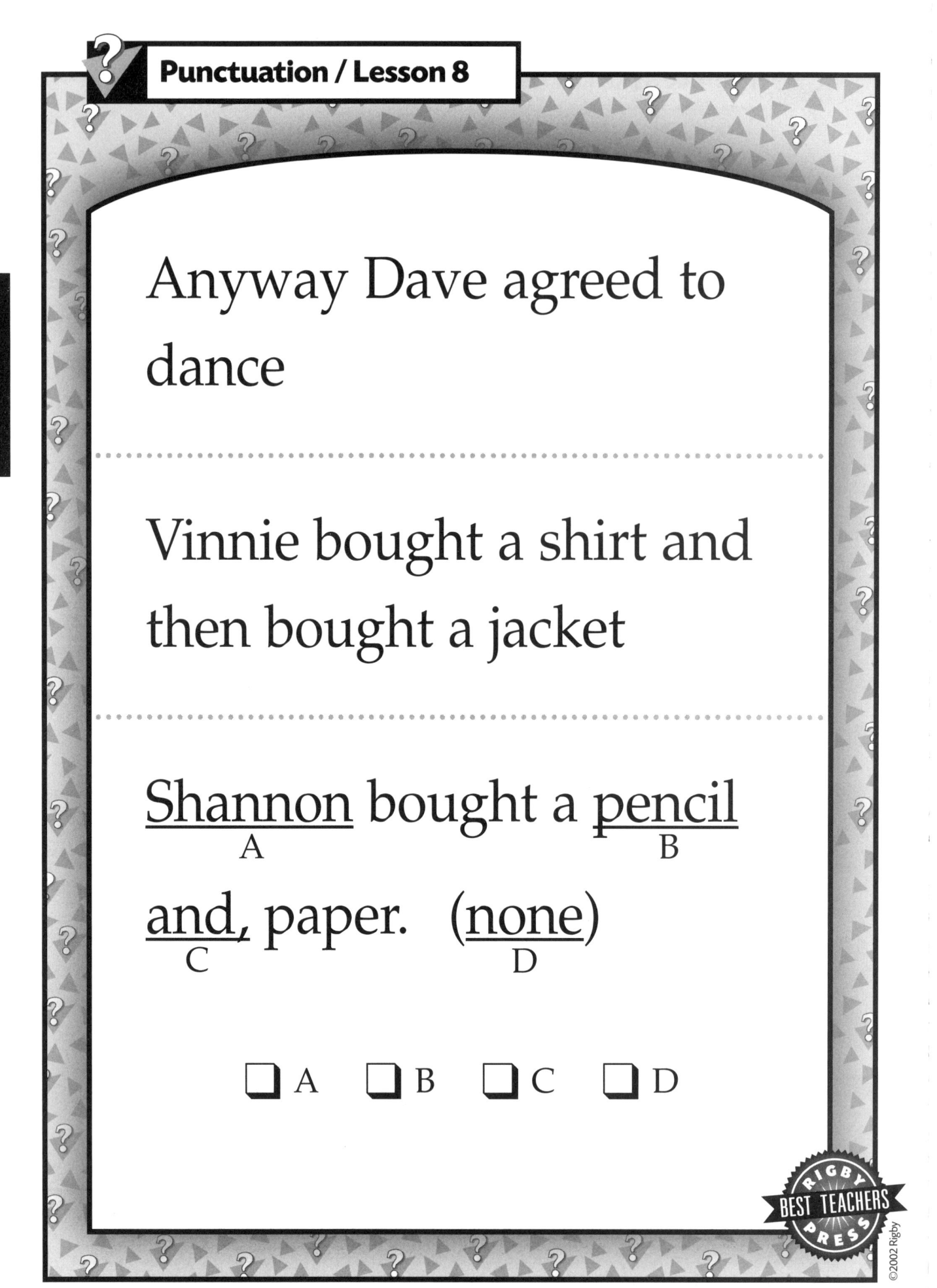

Anyway Dave agreed to dance

Vinnie bought a shirt and then bought a jacket

Shannon bought a pencil and, paper. (none)
 A   B
      C   D

☐ A   ☐ B   ☐ C   ☐ D

Punctuation / Lesson 9

Juan do you listen to W.S.T.V.

Linda that book is ours

Mrs. Jones, did you attend the P.T.A. meeting?
 A   B   C

(none)
  D

☐ A   ☐ B   ☐ C   ☐ D

Punctuation / Lesson 10

The students James John and Vicki failed the test

Were there many 100s on the spelling test

The fifth grade class won twenty five books.
     A   B   C

(none)
D

❏ A   ❏ B   ❏ C   ❏ D

Punctuation / Lesson 11

You ate two thirds of the cake exclaimed Jack

Cheryl asked Have you read Battle of the Giants yet

Mr. Juan Valo <u>wrote</u> the
         A
song <u>Mary's Dance</u> for the
         B
class <u>play.</u> (<u>none</u>)
      C   D

☐ A   ☐ B   ☐ C   ☐ D

Punctuation / Lesson 12

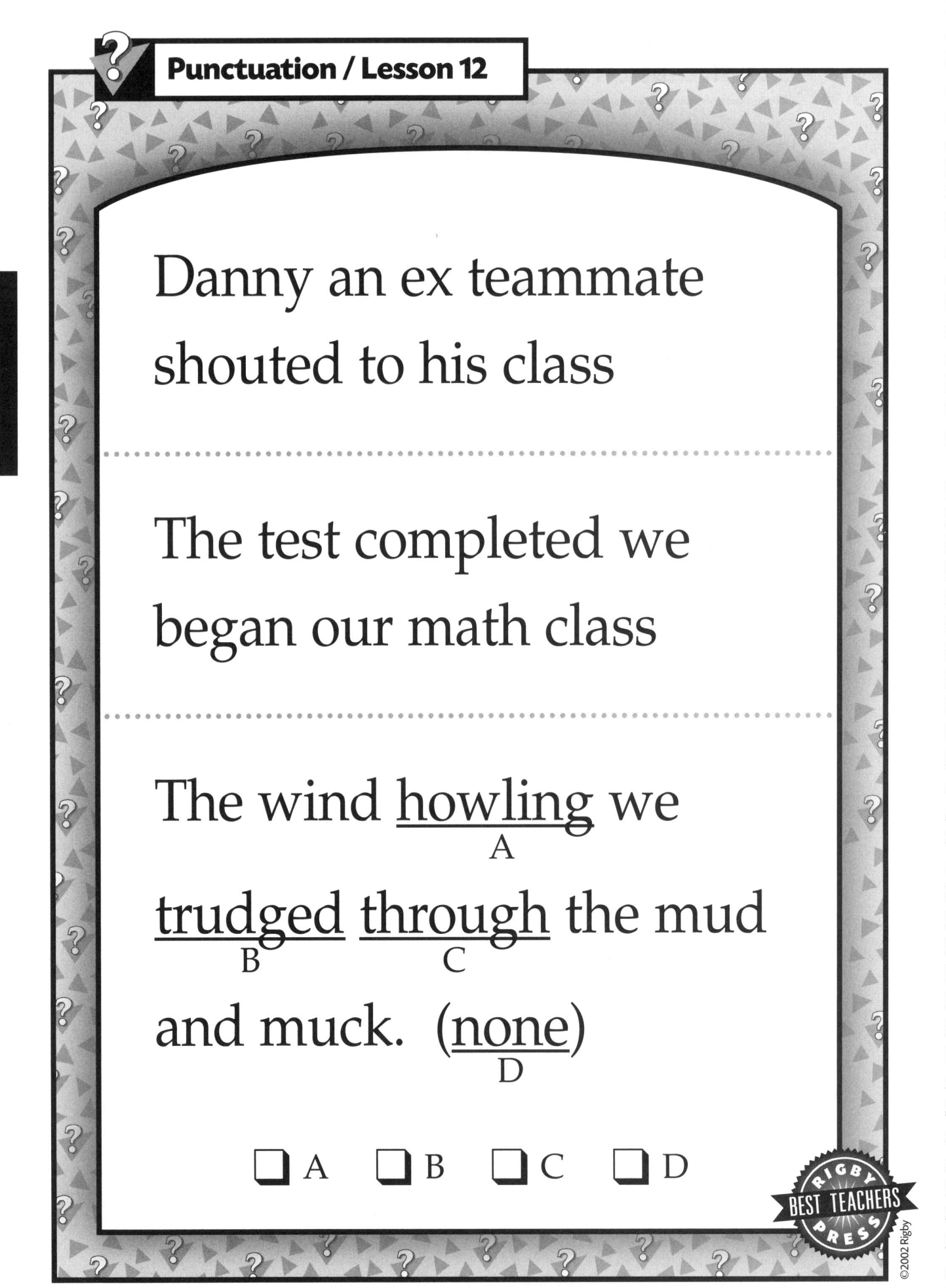

Danny an ex teammate shouted to his class

The test completed we began our math class

The wind <u>howling</u> we
             A
<u>trudged</u> <u>through</u> the mud
  B   C
and muck. (<u>none</u>)
              D

☐ A   ☐ B   ☐ C   ☐ D

Punctuation / Lesson 13

The math test was very hard therefore many students did not pass

Will you help me with my math and then will you help me with my spelling

Jane said, "I will help you with your math, and spelling." (none)
⠀⠀⠀⠀⠀A⠀⠀⠀⠀⠀⠀⠀⠀⠀⠀⠀⠀⠀⠀B⠀⠀⠀⠀⠀⠀⠀⠀⠀⠀C⠀⠀⠀⠀⠀⠀⠀⠀⠀⠀⠀D

☐ A ☐ B ☐ C ☐ D

Punctuation / Lesson 14

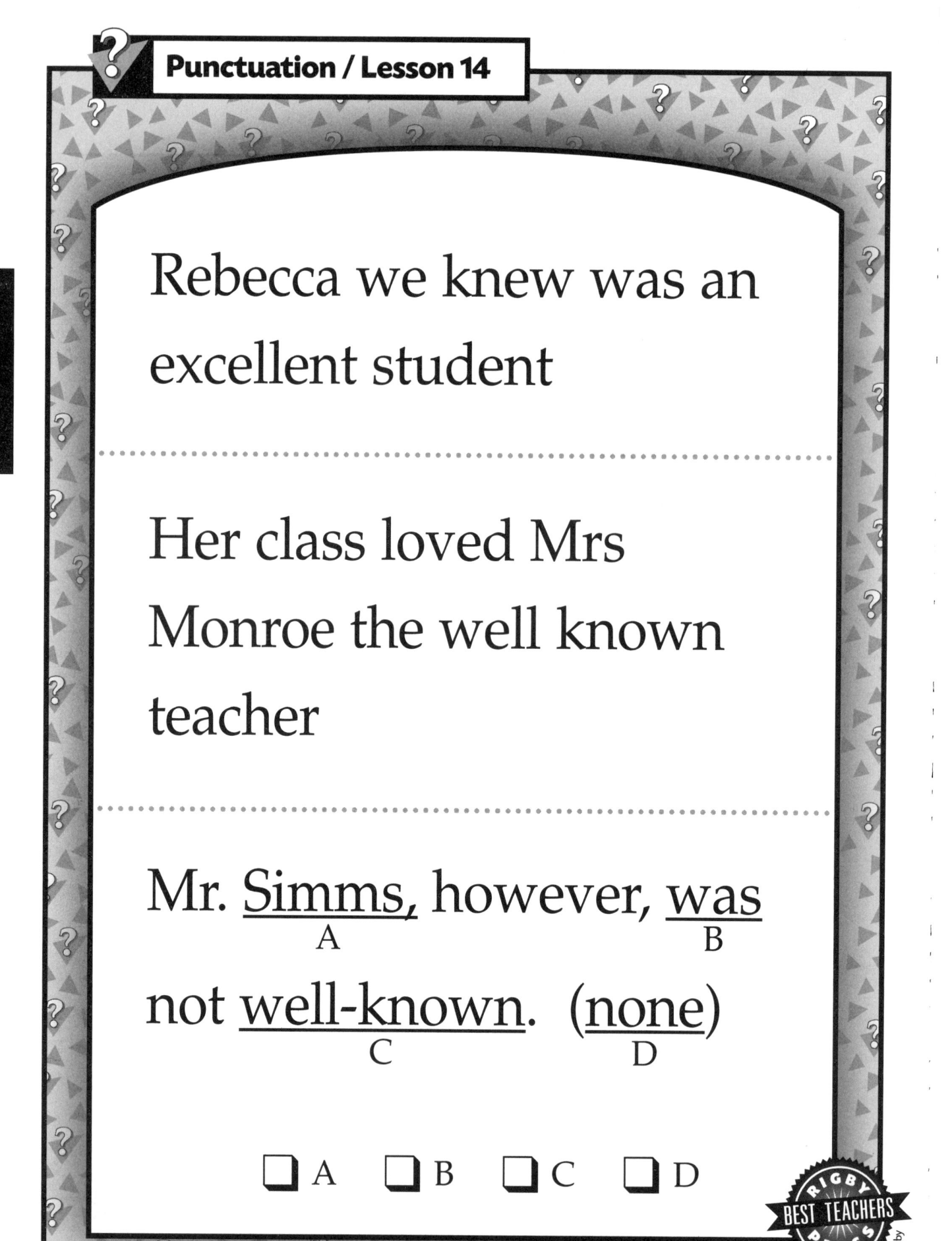

Rebecca we knew was an excellent student

Her class loved Mrs Monroe the well known teacher

Mr. Simms, however, was
     —A—   —B—
not well-known. (none)
    —C—   —D—

☐ A ☐ B ☐ C ☐ D

Punctuation / Lesson 15

If Jordan knew how to dance he would be the hit of the party

Greg would be the hit of the party if he knew how to dance

Margaret <u>will</u> study <u>hard,</u> if she wants to do well on the test<u>.</u> (<u>none</u>)
　　　　　A　　　　　B　　　　　　　　　　　　　　　　C　　　D

☐ A   ☐ B   ☐ C   ☐ D

Punctuation / Lesson 16

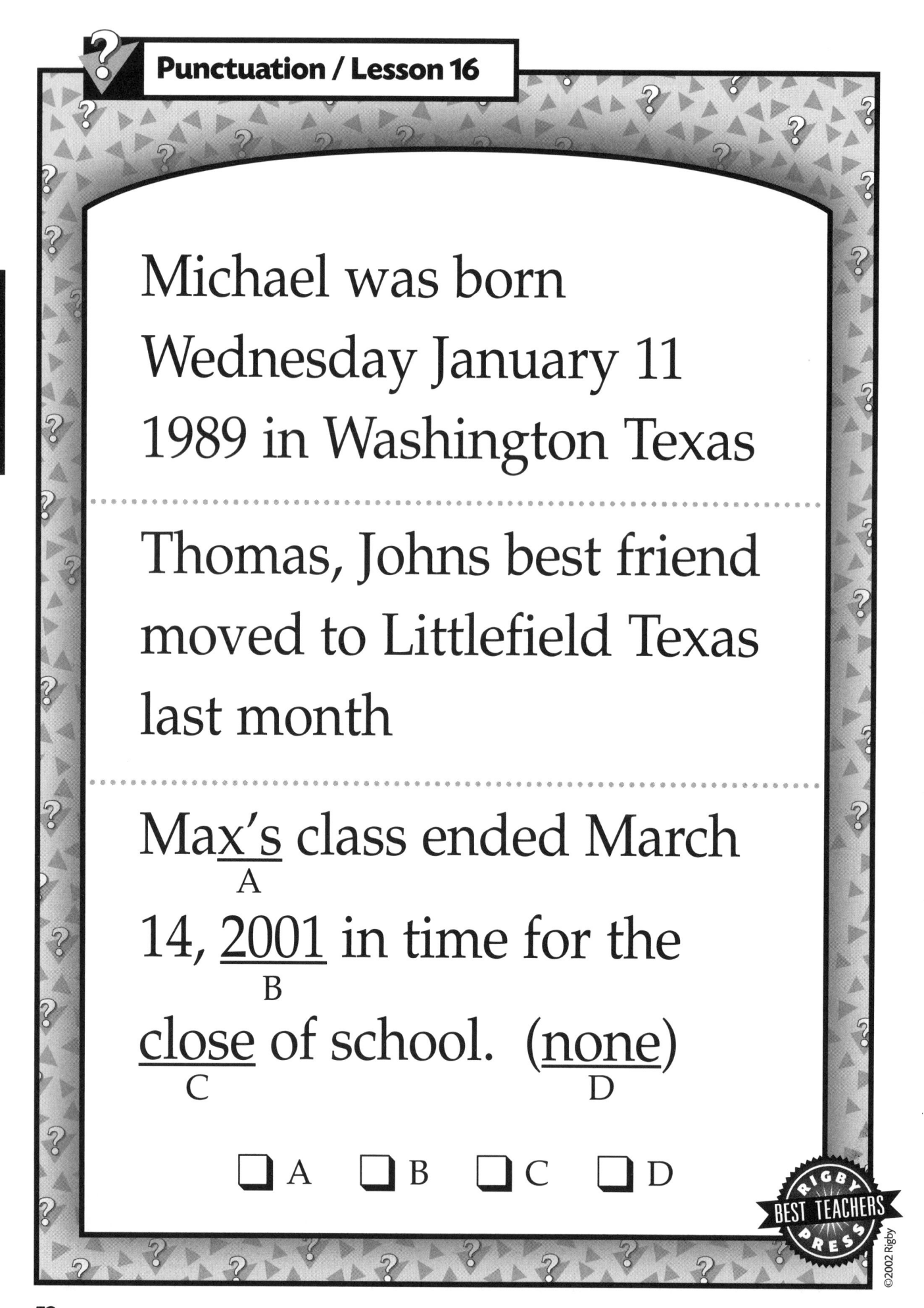

Michael was born Wednesday January 11 1989 in Washington Texas

Thomas, Johns best friend moved to Littlefield Texas last month

Ma<u>x's</u> class ended March
  A

14, <u>2001</u> in time for the
    B

<u>close</u> of school. (<u>none</u>)
 C   D

❏ A   ❏ B   ❏ C   ❏ D

Punctuation / Lesson 17

She likes to play two sports basketball and soccer

Do they have two pencils three books and one sheet of paper

Bill <u>has</u> three <u>kinds</u> of
    A   B
book<u>s:</u> math, science, and
   C
history. (<u>none</u>)
            D

❏ A   ❏ B   ❏ C   ❏ D

Punctuation / Lesson 18

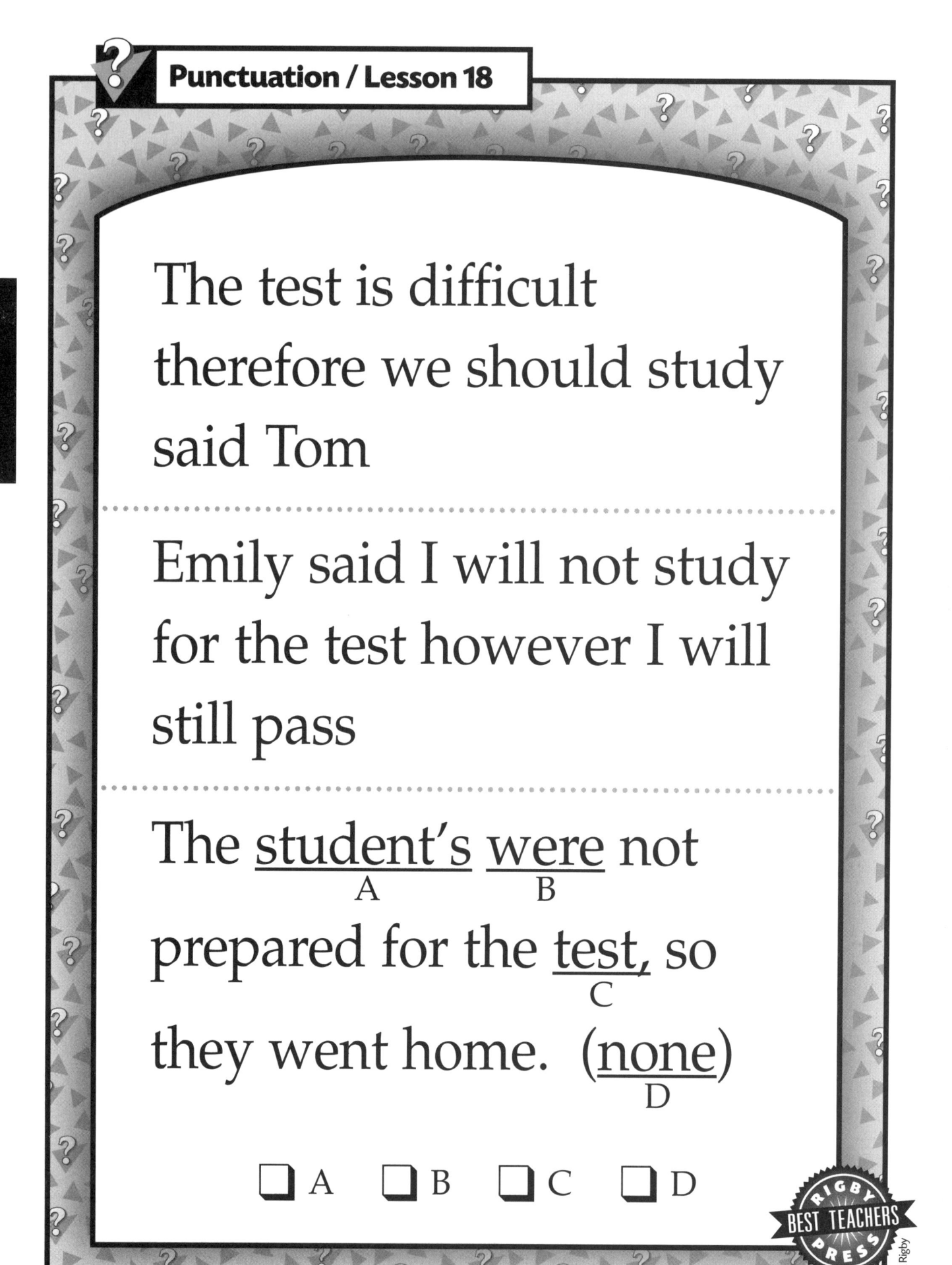

The test is difficult therefore we should study said Tom

Emily said I will not study for the test however I will still pass

The <u>student's</u> <u>were</u> not
     A   B

prepared for the <u>test,</u> so
               C

they went home. (<u>none</u>)
                  D

☐ A   ☐ B   ☐ C   ☐ D

Punctuation / Lesson 19

Would you please open your book

Sam asked Can you answer the question Nick

The <u>girls</u> asked, <u>"Who</u>
⎵   ⎵
A   B

baked the cherry <u>pie?</u>
C

(<u>none</u>)
D

☐ A   ☐ B   ☐ C   ☐ D

Punctuation / Lesson 20

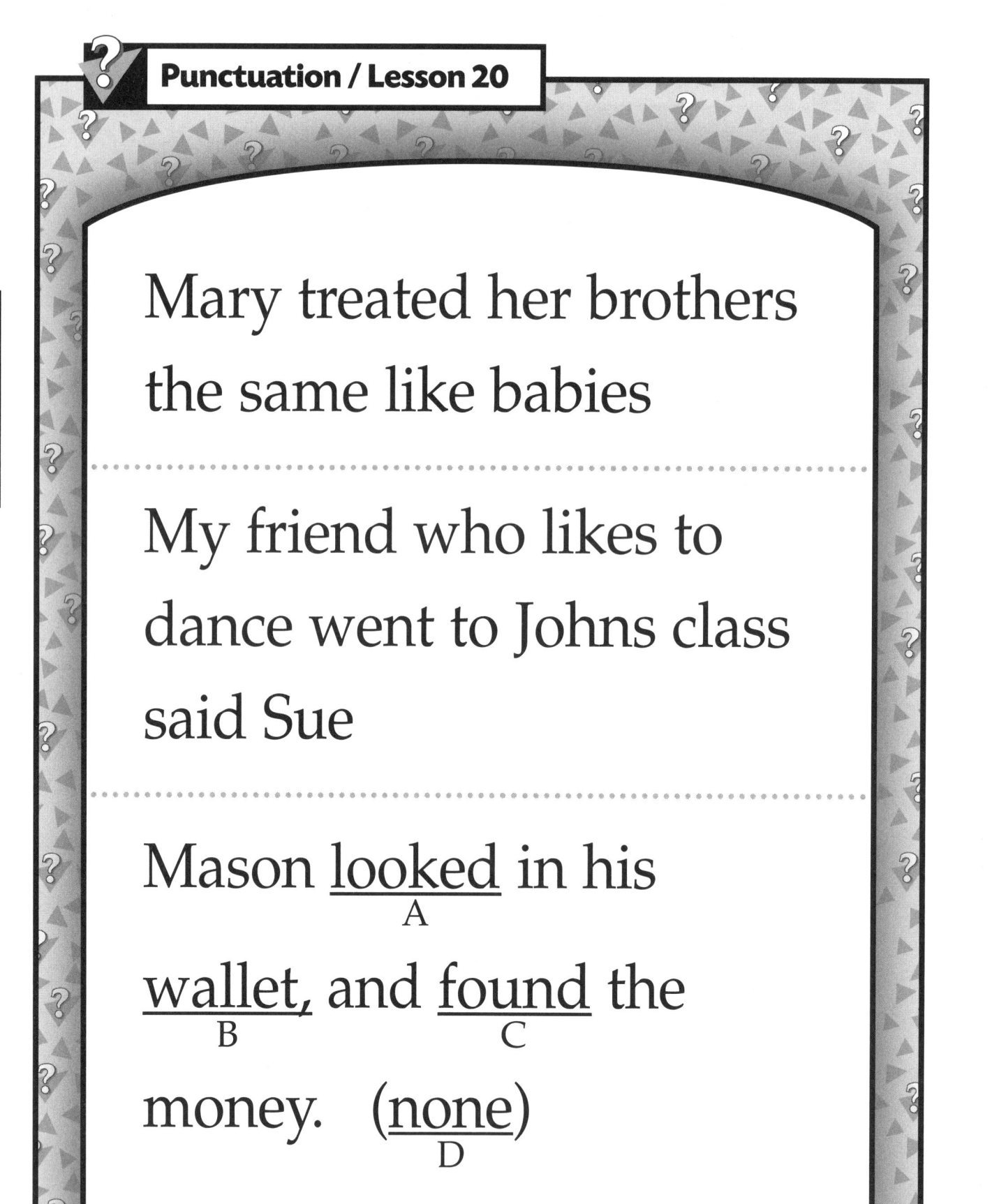

Mary treated her brothers the same like babies

My friend who likes to dance went to Johns class said Sue

Mason <u>looked</u> in his
      A
<u>wallet,</u> and <u>found</u> the
  B   C
money. (<u>none</u>)
              D

☐ A   ☐ B   ☐ C   ☐ D

Punctuation / Lesson 21

You should read Poes The Raven it is great

Should I write my report I wondered

"<u>Grab</u> the <u>dog,</u>" yelled
 A   B

John, "and hang <u>on.</u>"
                 C

(<u>none</u>)
  D

☐ A   ☐ B   ☐ C   ☐ D

Punctuation / Lesson 22

I want Omar remarked that old book

How are you Anna asked

He said <u>that</u> he <u>was going</u>
         A   B
home<u>.</u> (<u>none</u>)
    C   D

❏ A   ❏ B   ❏ C   ❏ D

Punctuation / Lesson 23

There are four 3s seven rs and five fourths in this problem

Karens friend was a freckle faced boy

He went to school, and took his test. (none)
    A   B   C   D

☐ A   ☐ B   ☐ C   ☐ D

Punctuation / Lesson 24

Laney a fifth grade student wants to join the math club instead of the science club

During the test students became nervous

Hello, how are you today?
   A   B   C

(none)
  D

❏ A   ❏ B   ❏ C   ❏ D

Punctuation / Lesson 25

Johns class ate cherry pie delicious cake and hot muffins

Dr Horaces car an old junk heap is parked on the street

Ramona's friend Juan is a short, shy young man.
   A   B   C
(none)
  D

☐ A   ☐ B   ☐ C   ☐ D

Punctuation / Lesson 26

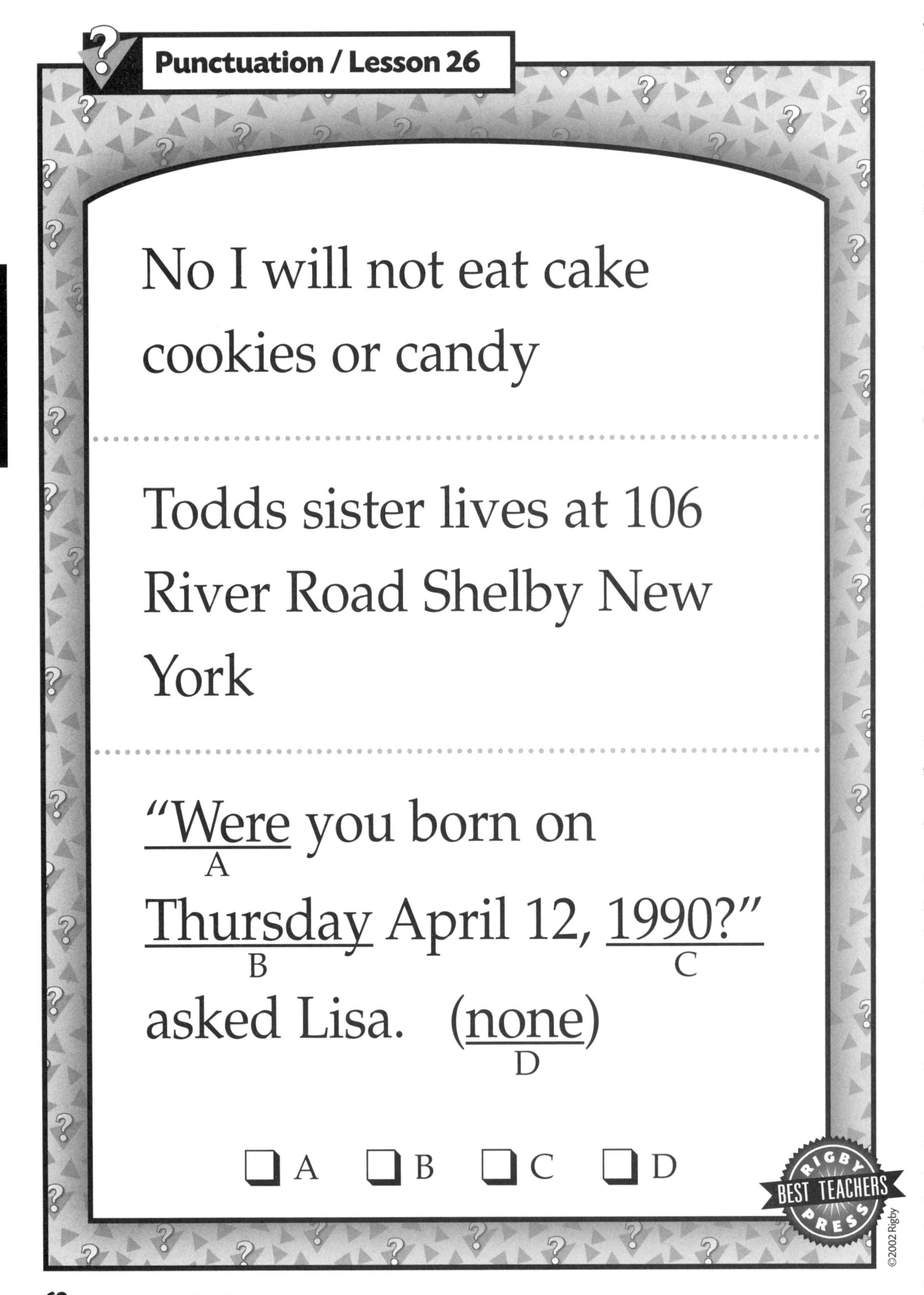

No I will not eat cake cookies or candy

Todds sister lives at 106 River Road Shelby New York

"Were you born on
 A
Thursday April 12, 1990?"
  B   C
asked Lisa. (none)
                D

☐ A   ☐ B   ☐ C   ☐ D

Punctuation / Lesson 27

Saras dog stood at the corner she would not move

Lets find its collar said John

While Liz <u>was</u> eating lunch
         A
with <u>Scott</u> Doug <u>walked</u> in.
     B   C
(<u>none</u>)
  D

❑ A   ❑ B   ❑ C   ❑ D

Punctuation / Lesson 28

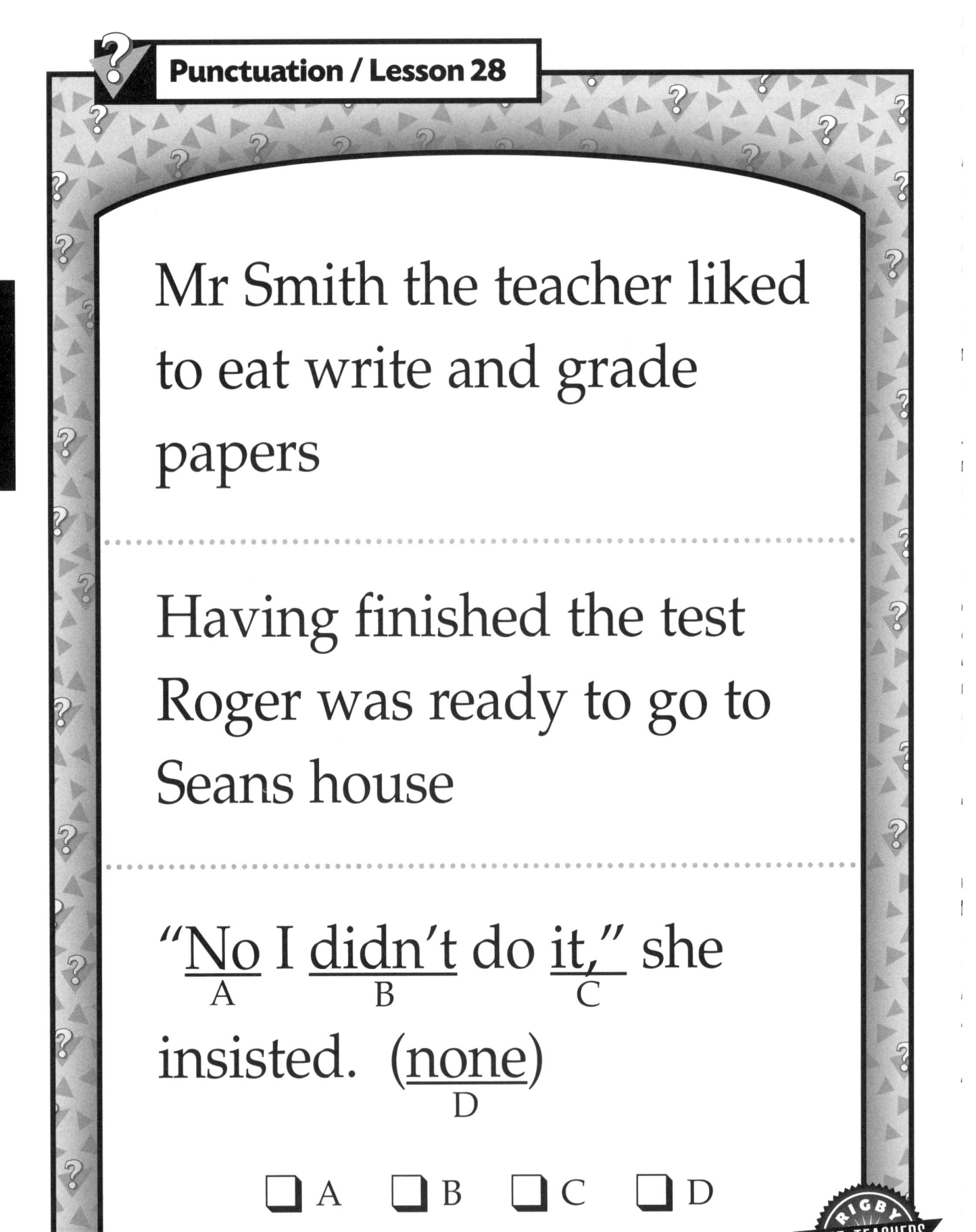

Mr Smith the teacher liked to eat write and grade papers

Having finished the test Roger was ready to go to Seans house

"No I didn't do it," she insisted. (none)
 A   B   C   D

☐ A ☐ B ☐ C ☐ D

Punctuation / Lesson 29

Toms sister I am sure will cook chicken pie bacon and eggs and spiced apple cake for dinner

It was a hot humid July night and I loved it

Mom <u>asked,</u> "<u>Arthur,</u> will you please wash the <u>dishes"?</u> (<u>none</u>)
     A   B   C   D

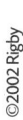

☐ A   ☐ B   ☐ C   ☐ D

Punctuation / Lesson 30

Its time to find Brians dog said Mark

Jonas has lost his book therefore he must buy a new one

School <u>is</u> <u>hard</u> but I like <u>it.</u>
　　　　A　　B　　　　　　　C

(<u>none</u>)
　D

☐ A　☐ B　☐ C　☐ D

Capitalization / Lesson 1

steven and i will read the book.

the class will begin on wednesday, may 3rd.

Mr. <u>Lamb</u>, our <u>Principal</u>,
     A   B
will speak to the <u>class</u>.
                      C
(<u>none</u>)
 D

☐ A   ☐ B   ☐ C   ☐ D

Capitalization / Lesson 2

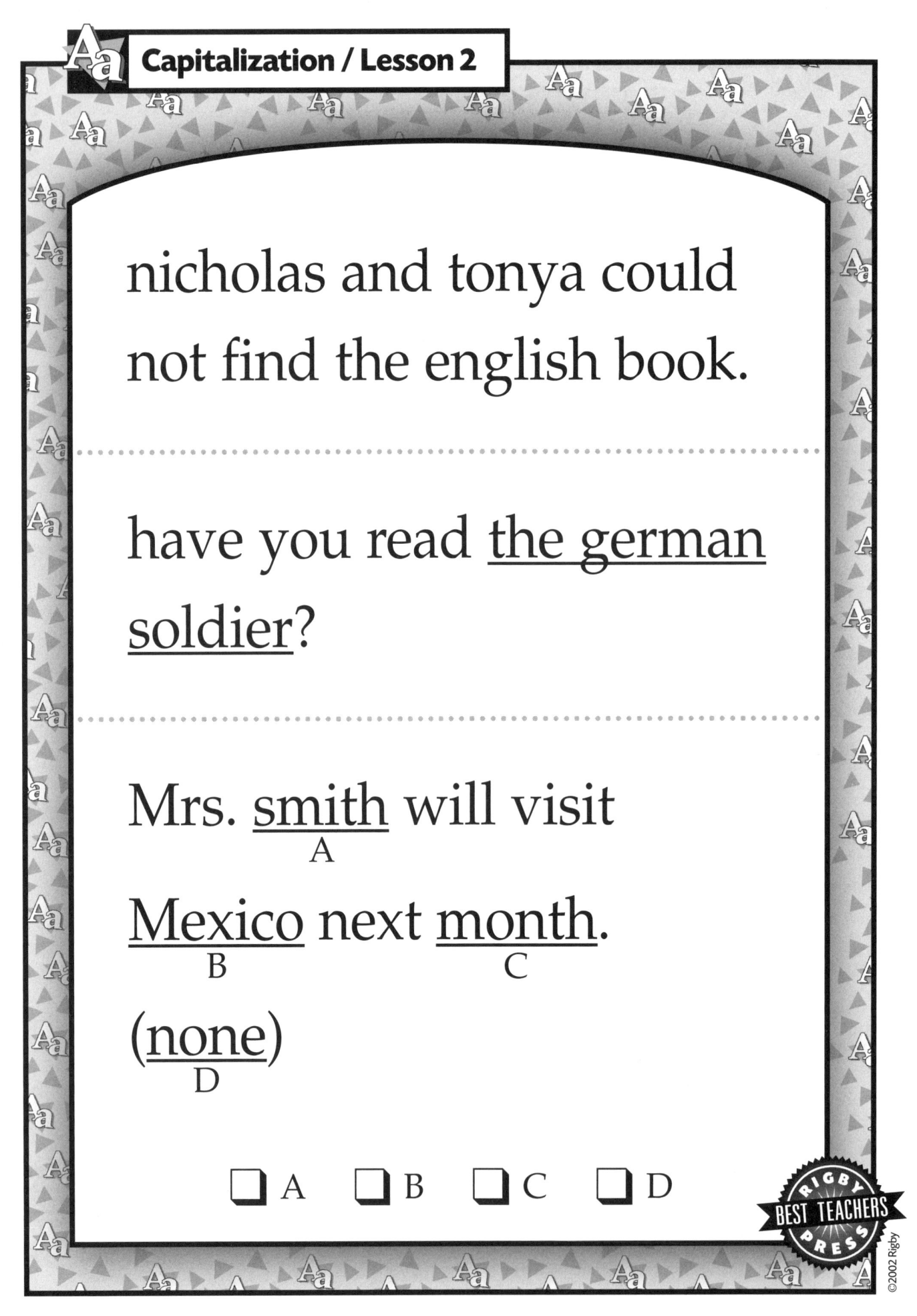

nicholas and tonya could not find the english book.

have you read the german soldier?

Mrs. smith will visit Mexico next month. (none)
     A   B   C   D

☐ A   ☐ B   ☐ C   ☐ D

Capitalization / Lesson 3

Juan would like to play in the world series for boston.

....

stuart and katherine will perform in the play <u>pinballs</u>.

....

Do you <u>speak</u> <u>English</u> or
      A   B

<u>spanish</u>? (<u>none</u>)
  C   D

☐ A   ☐ B   ☐ C   ☐ D

Capitalization / Lesson 4

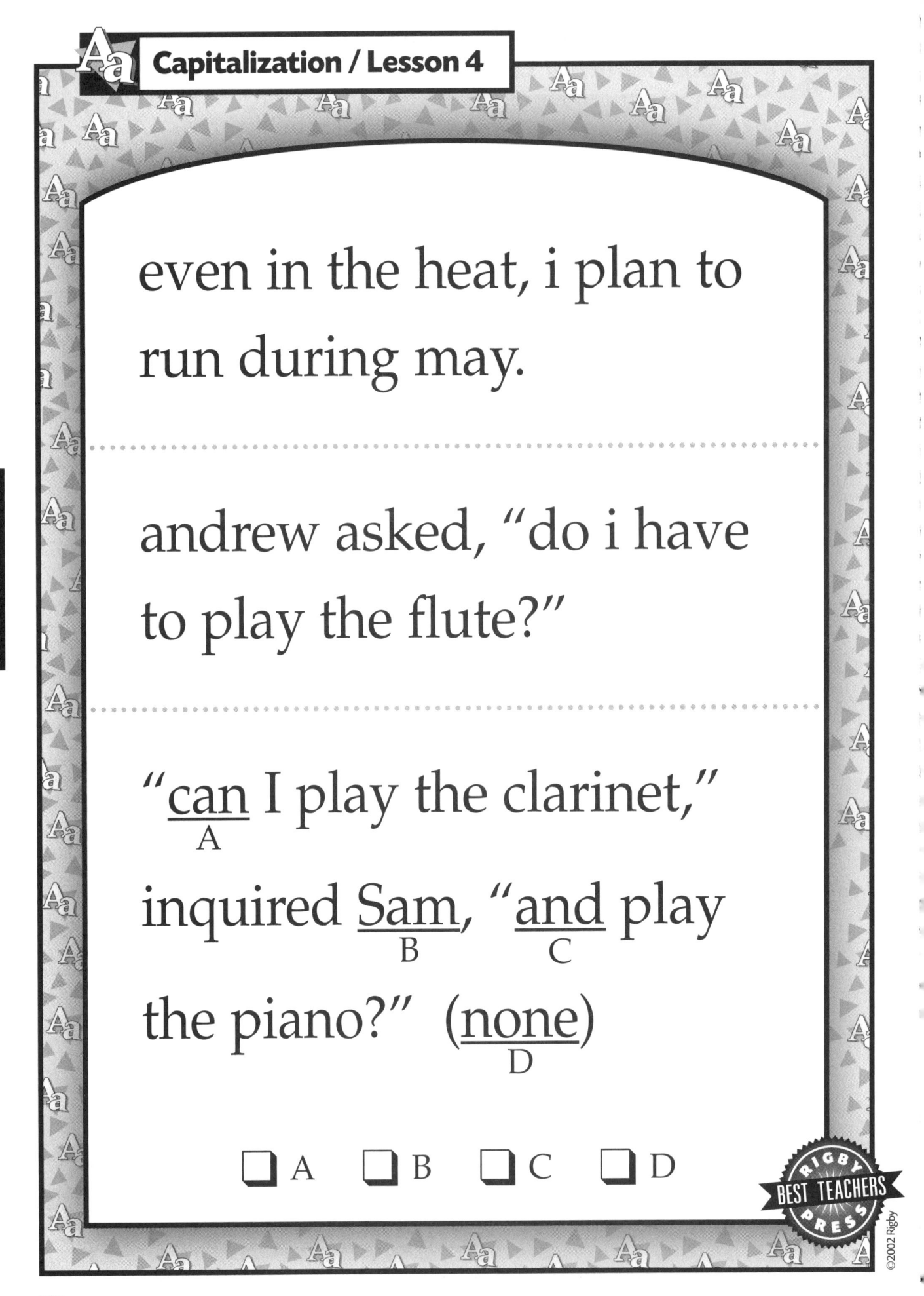

even in the heat, i plan to run during may.

andrew asked, "do i have to play the flute?"

"<u>can</u> I play the clarinet,"
  A

inquired <u>Sam</u>, "<u>and</u> play
        B   C

the piano?" (<u>none</u>)
              D

☐ A   ☐ B   ☐ C   ☐ D

Capitalization / Lesson 5

president lincoln lived in washington during the civil war.

paul will study the constitution for his history test.

The trip will begin thursday, April 7th. (none)
　　A　　　　　B　　　　C　　　　D

☐ A　　☐ B　　☐ C　　☐ D

Capitalization / Lesson 6

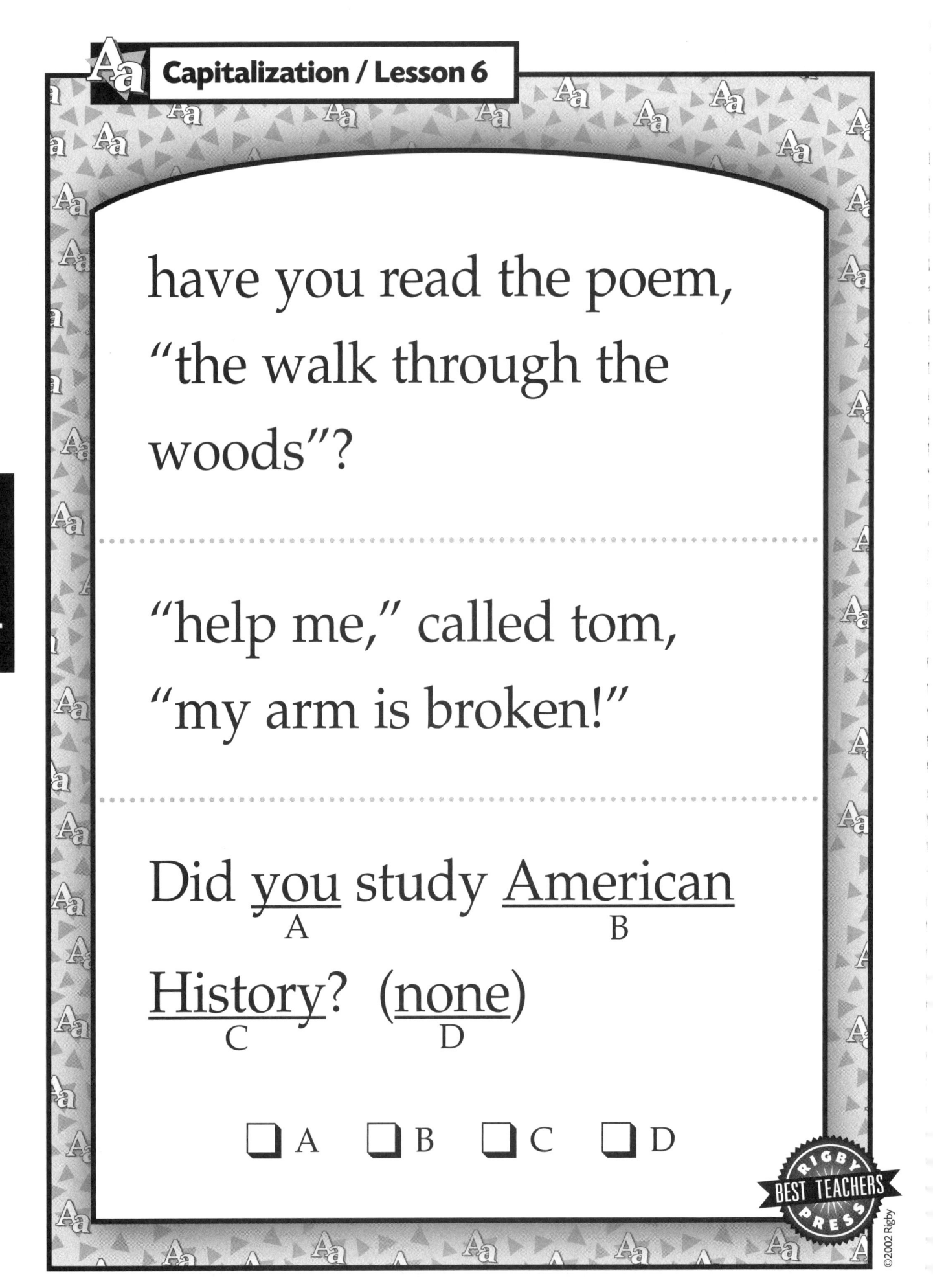

have you read the poem, "the walk through the woods"?

- -

"help me," called tom, "my arm is broken!"

- -

Did <u>you</u> study <u>American</u>
     A   B

<u>History</u>? (<u>none</u>)
  C   D

☐ A   ☐ B   ☐ C   ☐ D

Capitalization / Lesson 7

we will eat at grandma betty's house thursday, thanksgiving day.

jennifer parker, president of mode company, will visit during christmas vacation.

<u>She</u> enjoyed the visit with
 A

<u>President</u> <u>Smith</u>. (<u>none</u>)
   B   C   D

☐ A   ☐ B   ☐ C   ☐ D

Capitalization / Lesson 8

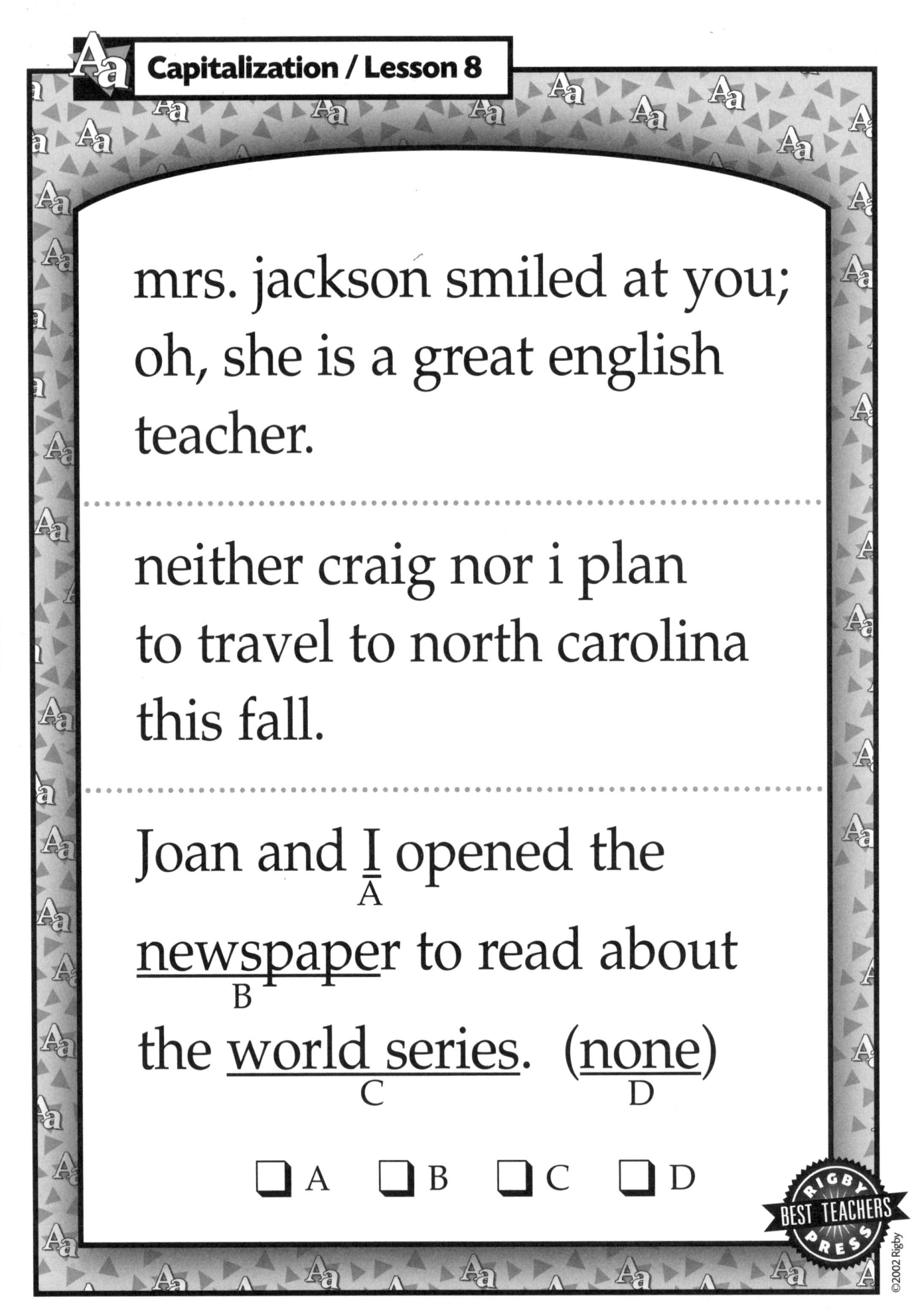

mrs. jackson smiled at you; oh, she is a great english teacher.

---

neither craig nor i plan to travel to north carolina this fall.

Joan and <u>I</u> opened the
    A
<u>newspaper</u> to read about
    B
the <u>world series</u>. (<u>none</u>)
       C   D

☐ A   ☐ B   ☐ C   ☐ D

Capitalization / Lesson 9

"don't leave the norwegian cruise ship," warned mark, "before it has dropped anchor."

do you enjoy your spanish, math, and english classes?

The <u>denver</u> basketball team <u>played</u> in <u>Chicago</u>.
  A   B   C
(<u>none</u>)
  D

☐ A   ☐ B   ☐ C   ☐ D

Capitalization / Lesson 10

tom and joseph's poem was published in <u>the news times</u>.

my favorite car is a ford taurus.

Mr. Walker <u>gave</u> his <u>english</u> class a <u>Christmas</u> party. (<u>none</u>)
  　　　　　A　　　　B　　　　　　　　C　　　　　　D

☐ A　☐ B　☐ C　☐ D

Capitalization / Lesson 11

mr. kay moved to texas from south dakota last may.

- - - - - - - - - - - - - - - -

they made a reservation at hotel south, 108 new street, portland, maine.

- - - - - - - - - - - - - - - -

For breakfast <u>we</u> ate ham
         A
and eggs, <u>Cereal</u>, and
              B
<u>sweet</u> rolls. (<u>none</u>)
  C   D

❏ A   ❏ B   ❏ C   ❏ D

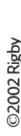

Capitalization / Lesson 12

miss carson prefers chicago to new york.

mike asked, "do you know the words to 'america the beautiful'?"

Jessica saw mayor Mullins eating breakfast at Don's Donuts. (none)
  A   B   C   D

❏ A   ❏ B   ❏ C   ❏ D

Capitalization / Lesson 13

julie and i were shopping at beth's boutique for a graduation dress.

our street has become so busy we are moving to elm street.

Next <u>saturday</u> we <u>will</u>
      A   B
study for our <u>English</u> test.
                 C
(<u>none</u>)
  D

❑ A   ❑ B   ❑ C   ❑ D

Capitalization / Lesson 14

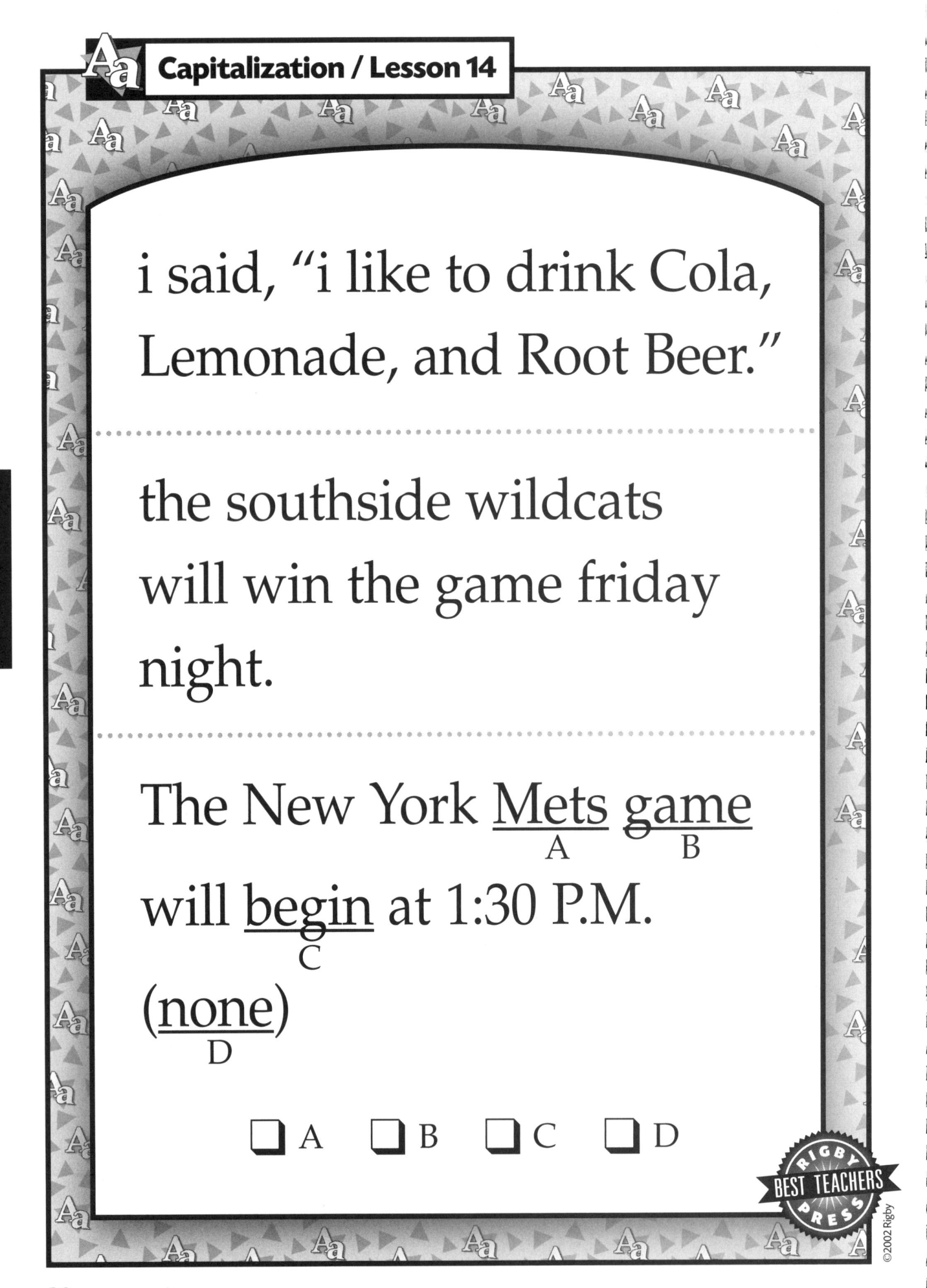

i said, "i like to drink Cola, Lemonade, and Root Beer."

....

the southside wildcats will win the game friday night.

....

The New York <u>Mets</u> <u>game</u>
          A   B
will <u>begin</u> at 1:30 P.M.
     C
(<u>none</u>)
  D

☐ A ☐ B ☐ C ☐ D

Capitalization / Lesson 15

after school, mom asked me to finish my english homework.

todd fisher asked his mom to pick him up at dyler middle school.

Hanes <u>mall</u> will be open
      A
late during the <u>January</u>
                    B
<u>holidays</u>. (<u>none</u>)
   C   D

☐ A ☐ B ☐ C ☐ D

Capitalization / Lesson 16

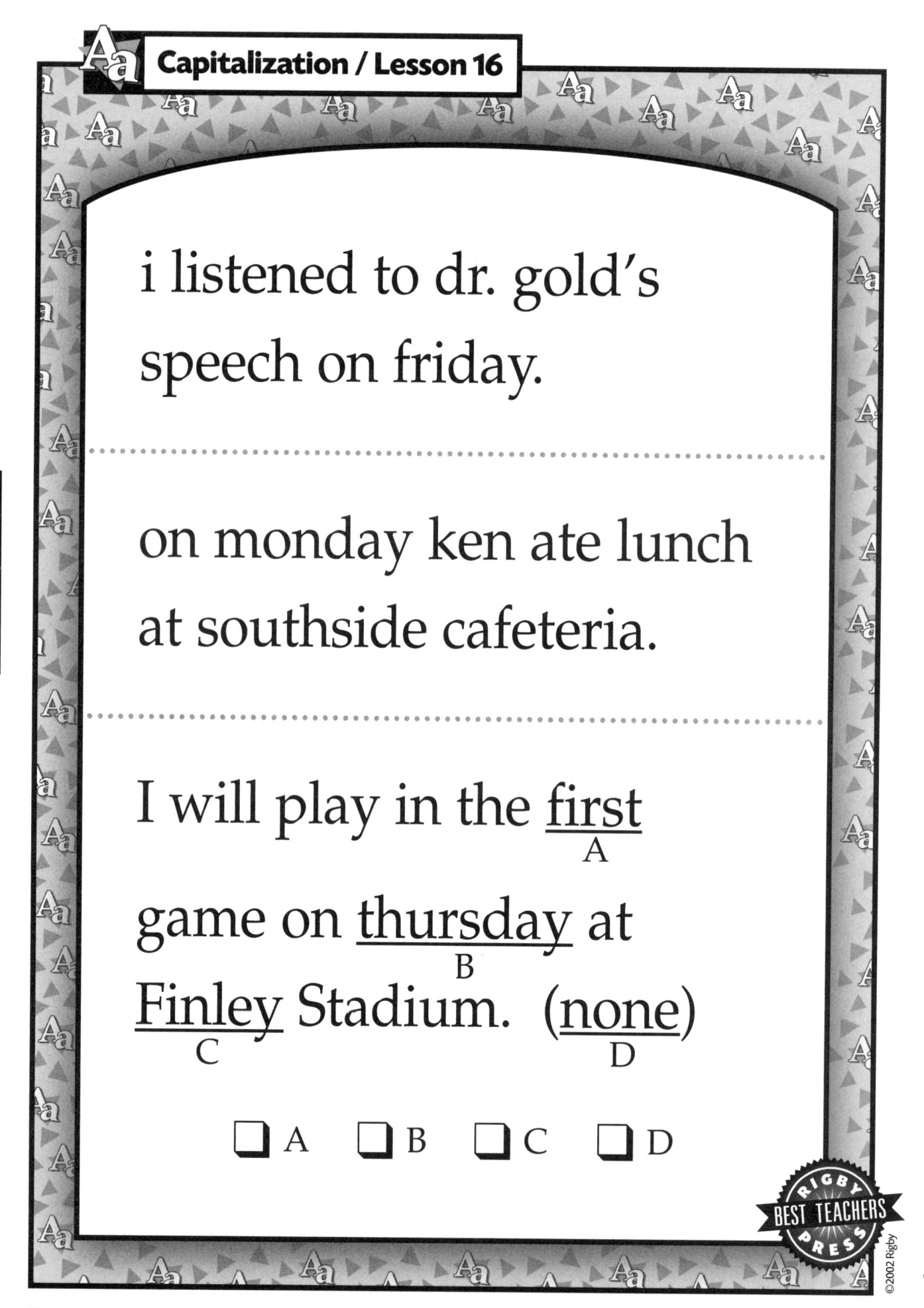

i listened to dr. gold's speech on friday.

on monday ken ate lunch at southside cafeteria.

I will play in the <u>first</u> game on <u>thursday</u> at <u>Finley</u> Stadium. (<u>none</u>)
          A   B   C   D

❏ A   ❏ B   ❏ C   ❏ D

Capitalization / Lesson 17

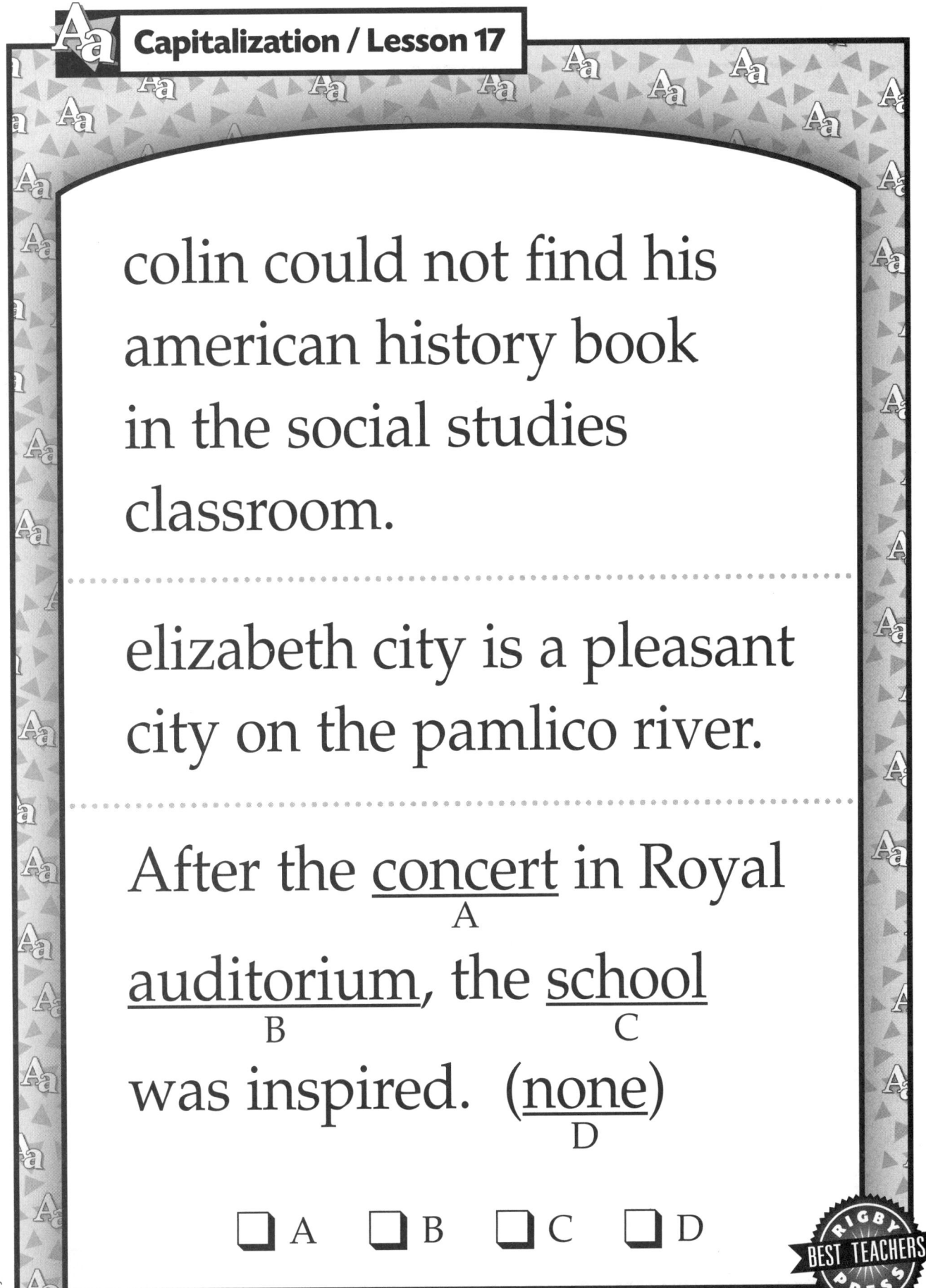

colin could not find his american history book in the social studies classroom.

---

elizabeth city is a pleasant city on the pamlico river.

After the <u>concert</u> in Royal
         A
<u>auditorium</u>, the <u>school</u>
    B   C
was inspired. (<u>none</u>)
                   D

☐ A   ☐ B   ☐ C   ☐ D

Capitalization / Lesson 18

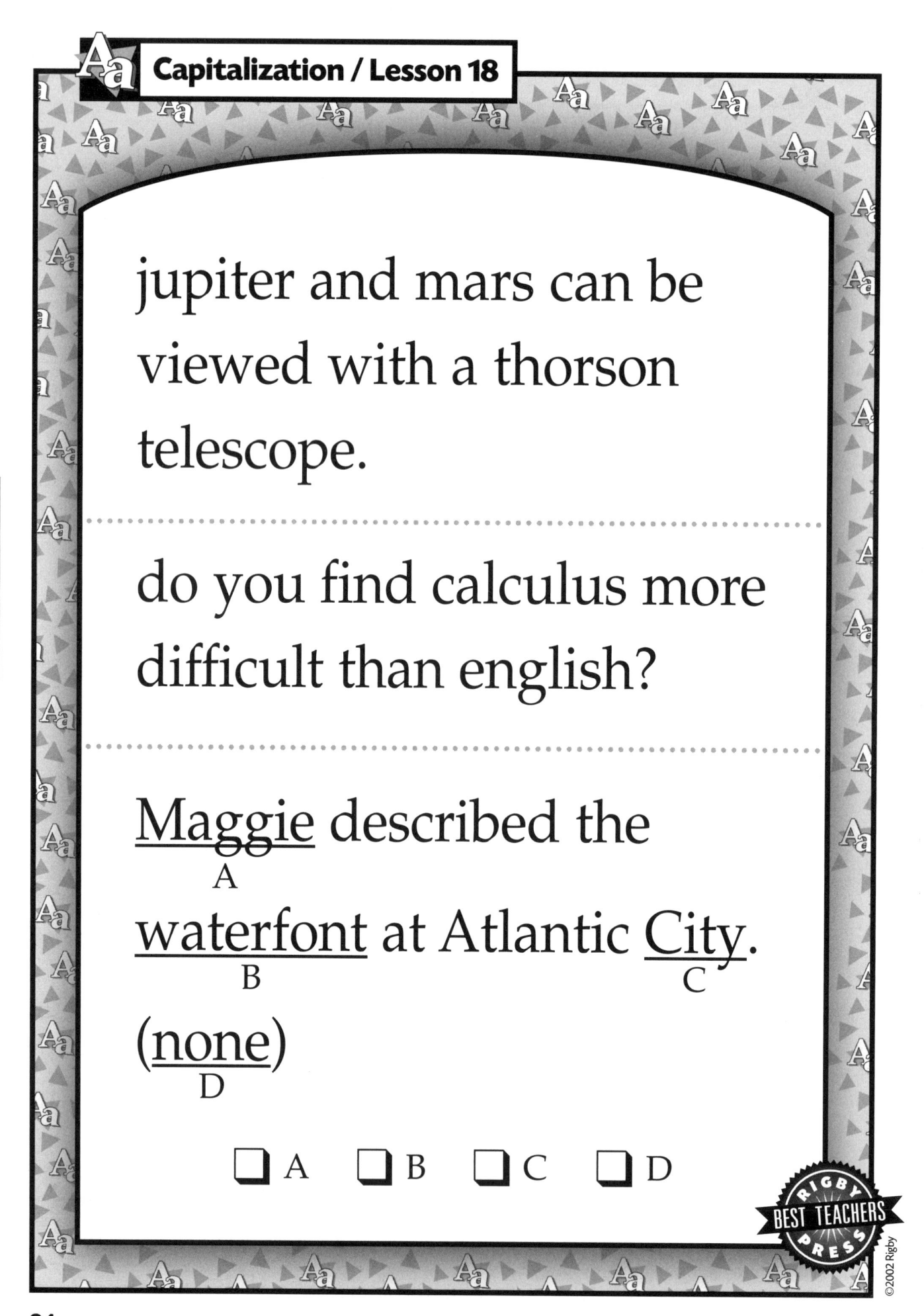

jupiter and mars can be viewed with a thorson telescope.

do you find calculus more difficult than english?

Maggie described the
　A
waterfont at Atlantic City.
　B　　　　　　　　　　C
(none)
　D

☐ A ☐ B ☐ C ☐ D

Capitalization / Lesson 19

"have you visited nasa in florida?" asked sue.

greg and steven read the poem "sleeping in the classroom" in english class.

"Creating Landscapes with Art" is an interesting poem. (none)
　　　　　 A　　B　　　　　　　　　　　C　　　D

☐ A　☐ B　☐ C　☐ D

Capitalization / Lesson 20

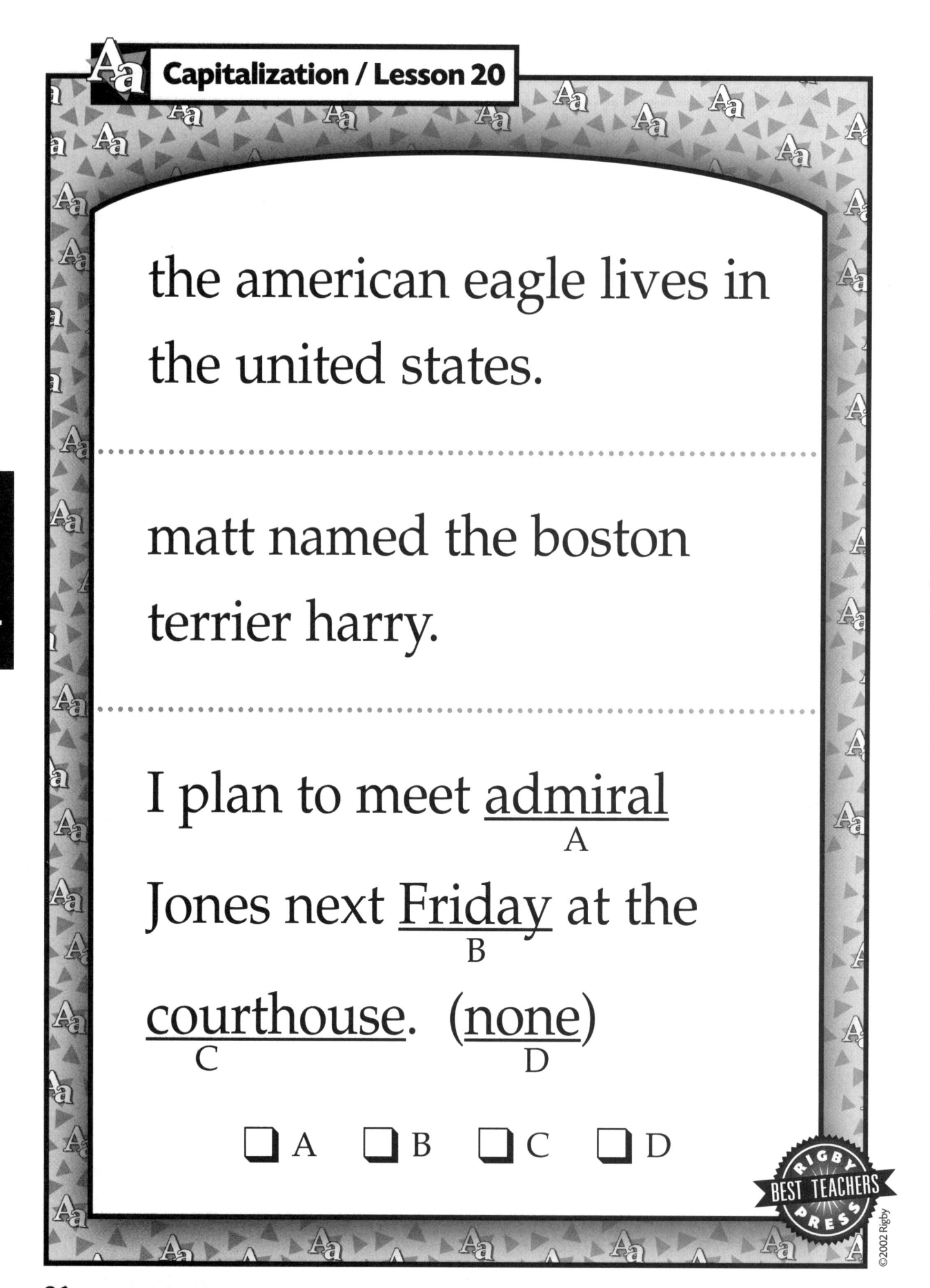

the american eagle lives in the united states.

---

matt named the boston terrier harry.

I plan to meet <u>admiral</u> Jones next <u>Friday</u> at the
　　　　　　　　　A　　　　　　　　B
<u>courthouse</u>. (<u>none</u>)
　　C　　　　　　D

☐ A　☐ B　☐ C　☐ D

Capitalization / Lesson 21

i saw mom talking to senator simms.

---

the class will plan a trip to the west next spring.

The <u>spring</u> breeze <u>comes</u>
     A   B
from the <u>west</u>. (<u>none</u>)
          C   D

☐ A   ☐ B   ☐ C   ☐ D

Capitalization / Lesson 22

carmen and i would like to join the girl scouts of america next fall.

......

the spanish-speaking students enjoyed gelatin.

......

Last <u>march</u>, our <u>French</u>
     A   B

teacher gave us a <u>spring</u>
                         C

party. (<u>none</u>)
        D

❏ A   ❏ B   ❏ C   ❏ D

Capitalization / Lesson 23

william enjoyed watching tv when he visited canada and mexico.

"did tom eat at the italian restaurant?" asked wayne.

It <u>often</u> rains <u>west</u> of the
    A   B
Red <u>river</u>. (<u>none</u>)
     C   D

☐ A ☐ B ☐ C ☐ D

Capitalization / Lesson 24

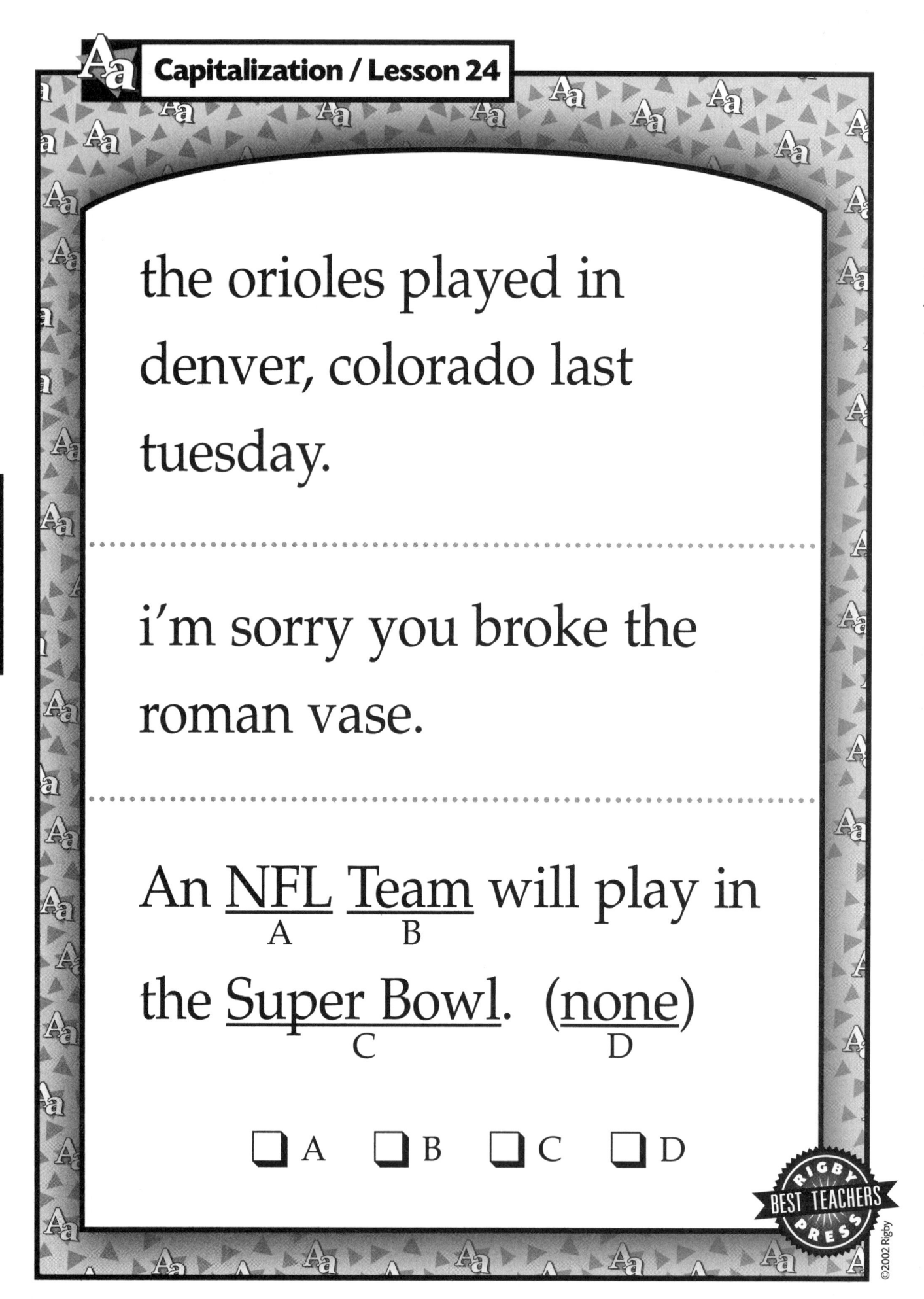

the orioles played in denver, colorado last tuesday.

....

i'm sorry you broke the roman vase.

....

An <u>NFL</u> <u>Team</u> will play in the <u>Super Bowl</u>. (<u>none</u>)
　　A　　B　　　　　　　C　　　　D

☐ A　☐ B　☐ C　☐ D

Capitalization / Lesson 25

my friend admiral hailey wanted to become a general.

i saw my mother and father shopping at harvey mall.

The <u>Detroit Pistons</u> <u>Team</u>
       A   B
will play in <u>Dallas</u>. (<u>none</u>)
              C   D

☐ A ☐ B ☐ C ☐ D

Capitalization / Lesson 26

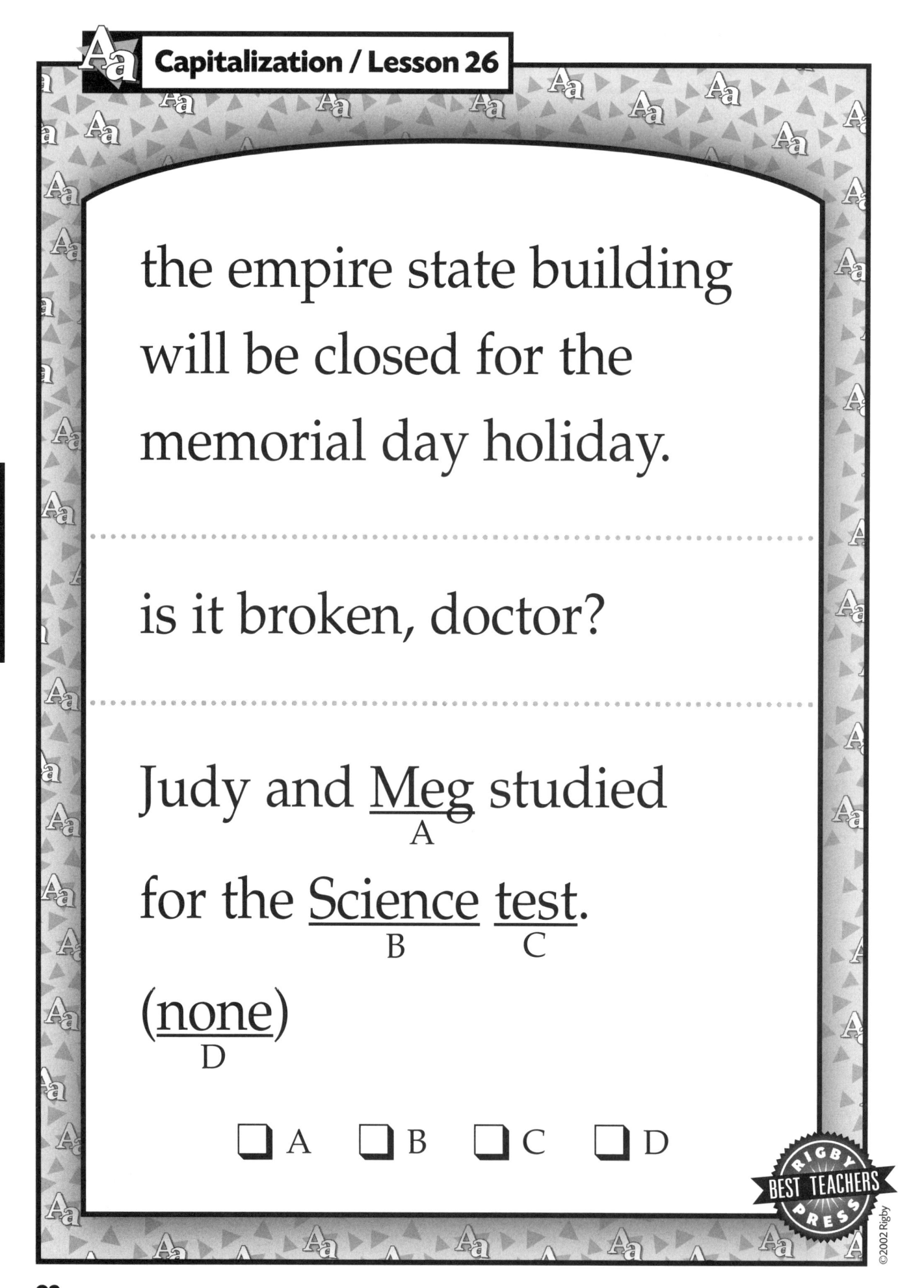

the empire state building will be closed for the memorial day holiday.

....

is it broken, doctor?

....

Judy and <u>Meg</u> studied
         A
for the <u>Science</u> <u>test</u>.
           B   C
(<u>none</u>)
   D

☐ A   ☐ B   ☐ C   ☐ D

Capitalization / Lesson 27

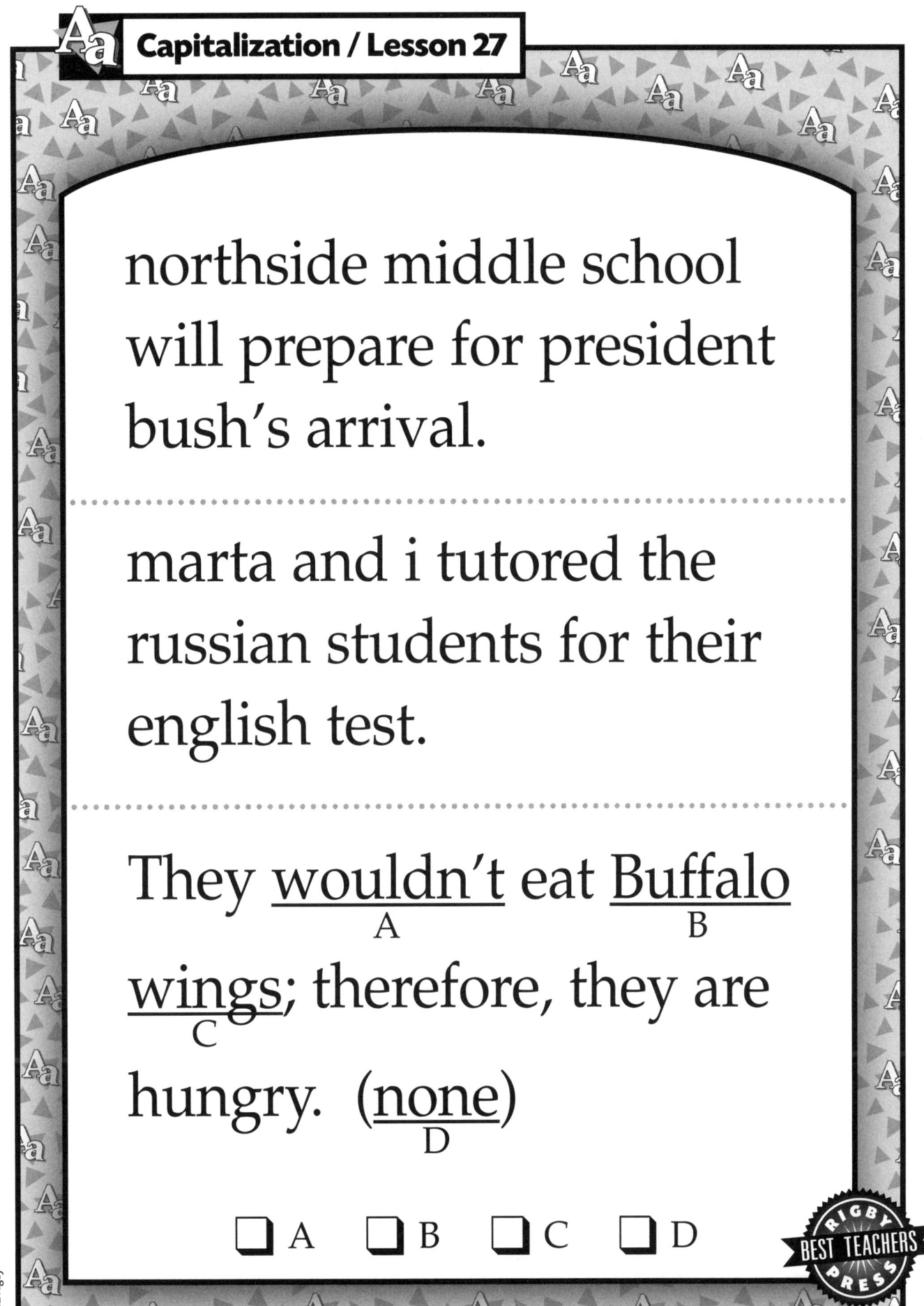

northside middle school will prepare for president bush's arrival.

marta and i tutored the russian students for their english test.

They <u>wouldn't</u> eat <u>Buffalo</u>
     A   B

<u>wings</u>; therefore, they are
 C

hungry. (<u>none</u>)
        D

☐ A   ☐ B   ☐ C   ☐ D

Capitalization / Lesson 28

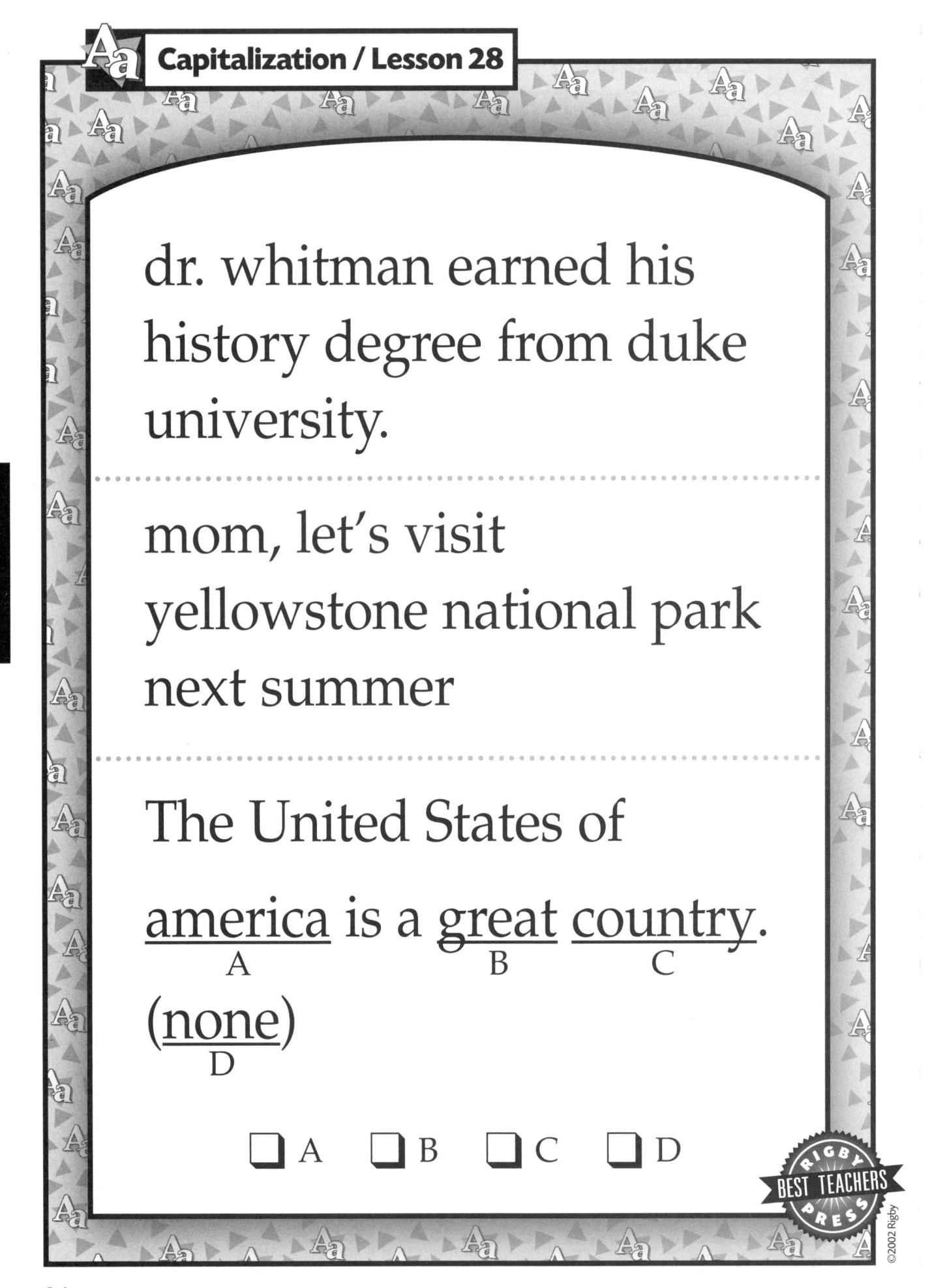

dr. whitman earned his history degree from duke university.

mom, let's visit yellowstone national park next summer

The United States of america is a great country.
　　　　　　　　　　A　　　　　　B　　　C
(none)
　D

☐ A ☐ B ☐ C ☐ D

Capitalization / Lesson 29

the manager's desk was covered with american beauty roses.

jake will visit south america and canada next april.

Will you help <u>me</u> pack for
           A
my <u>Alaskan</u> vacation,
      B
<u>mom</u>? (<u>none</u>)
 C   D

☐ A ☐ B ☐ C ☐ D

Capitalization / Lesson 30

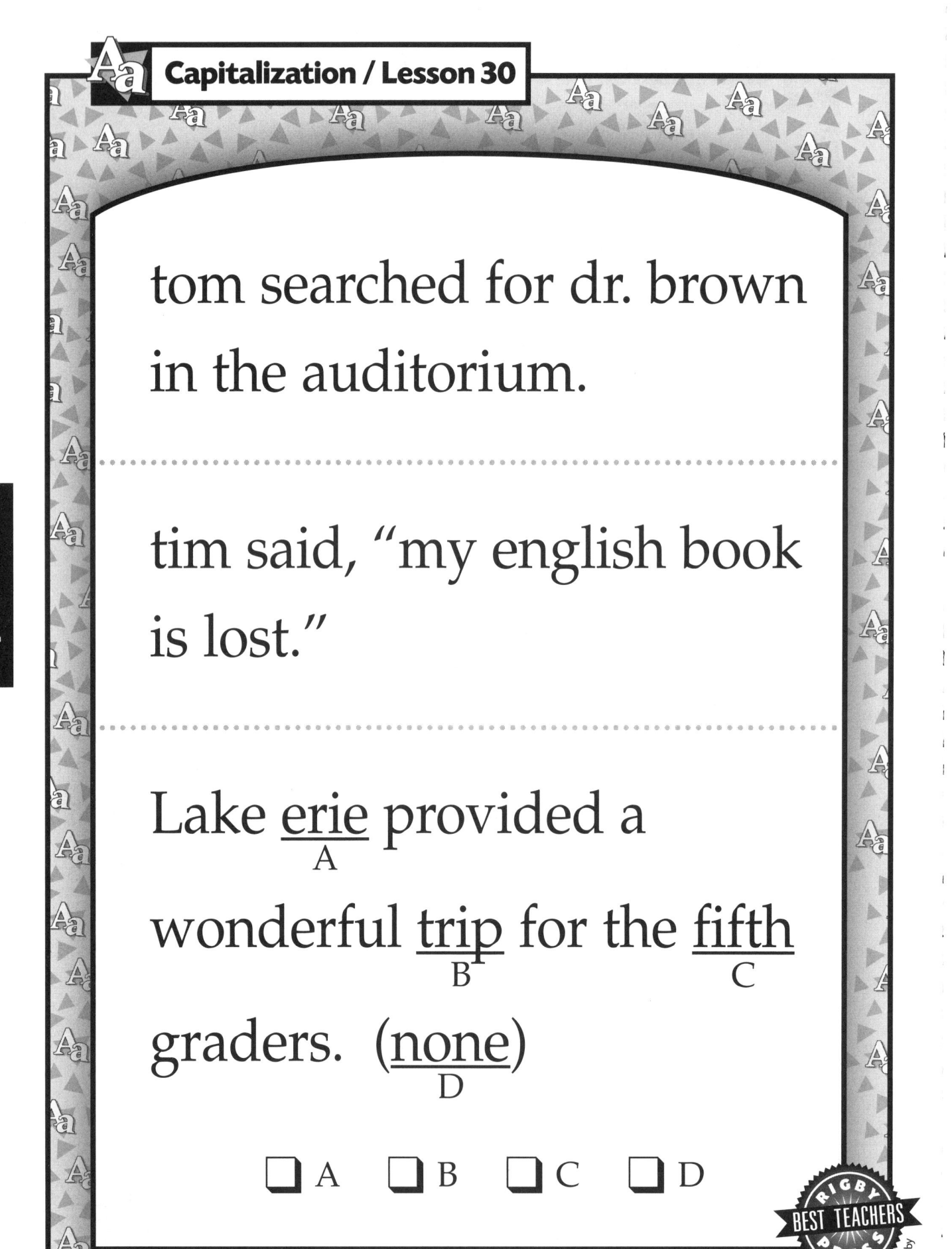

tom searched for dr. brown in the auditorium.

tim said, "my english book is lost."

Lake <u>erie</u> provided a wonderful <u>trip</u> for the <u>fifth</u> graders. (<u>none</u>)
     A   B   C   D

❏ A   ❏ B   ❏ C   ❏ D

Spelling / Lesson 1

The gril had lovly brown hair.

Tom wants to go to his frist class.

He did not <u>know</u> the
              A
<u>anser</u> to the <u>science</u>
B   C
question. (<u>none</u>)
           D

❏ A   ❏ B   ❏ C   ❏ D

Spelling / Lesson 2

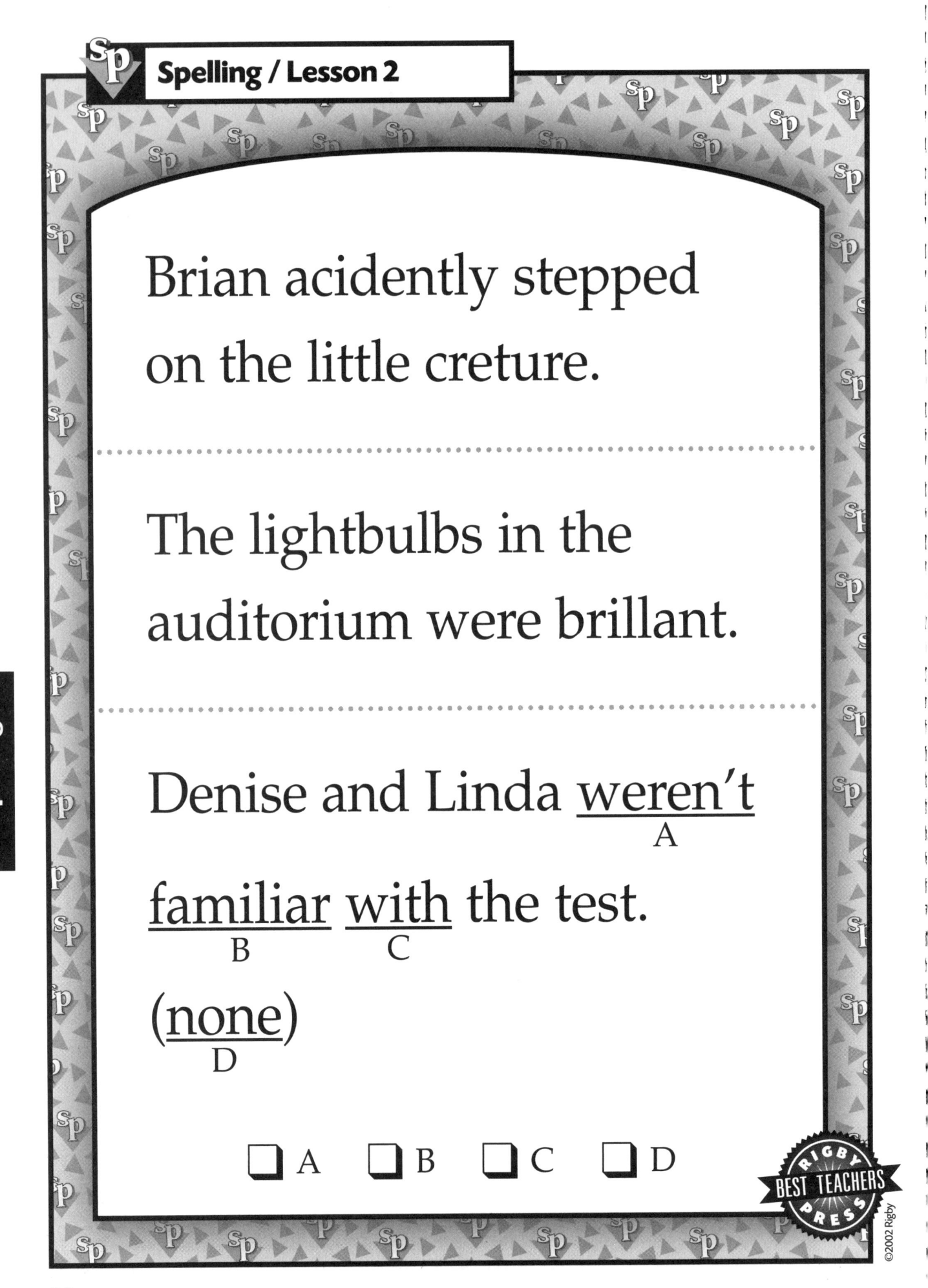

Brian acidently stepped on the little creture.

The lightbulbs in the auditorium were brillant.

Denise and Linda <u>weren't</u> <u>familiar</u> <u>with</u> the test. (<u>none</u>)
                    A
  B   C   D

☐ A   ☐ B   ☐ C   ☐ D

Spelling / Lesson 3

Chris rote a poem for his assignmint.

She likes arithmatic alot.

The <u>fiery</u> <u>building</u> was <u>scarey</u>. (<u>none</u>)
    A   B   C   D

☐ A ☐ B ☐ C ☐ D

Spelling / Lesson 4

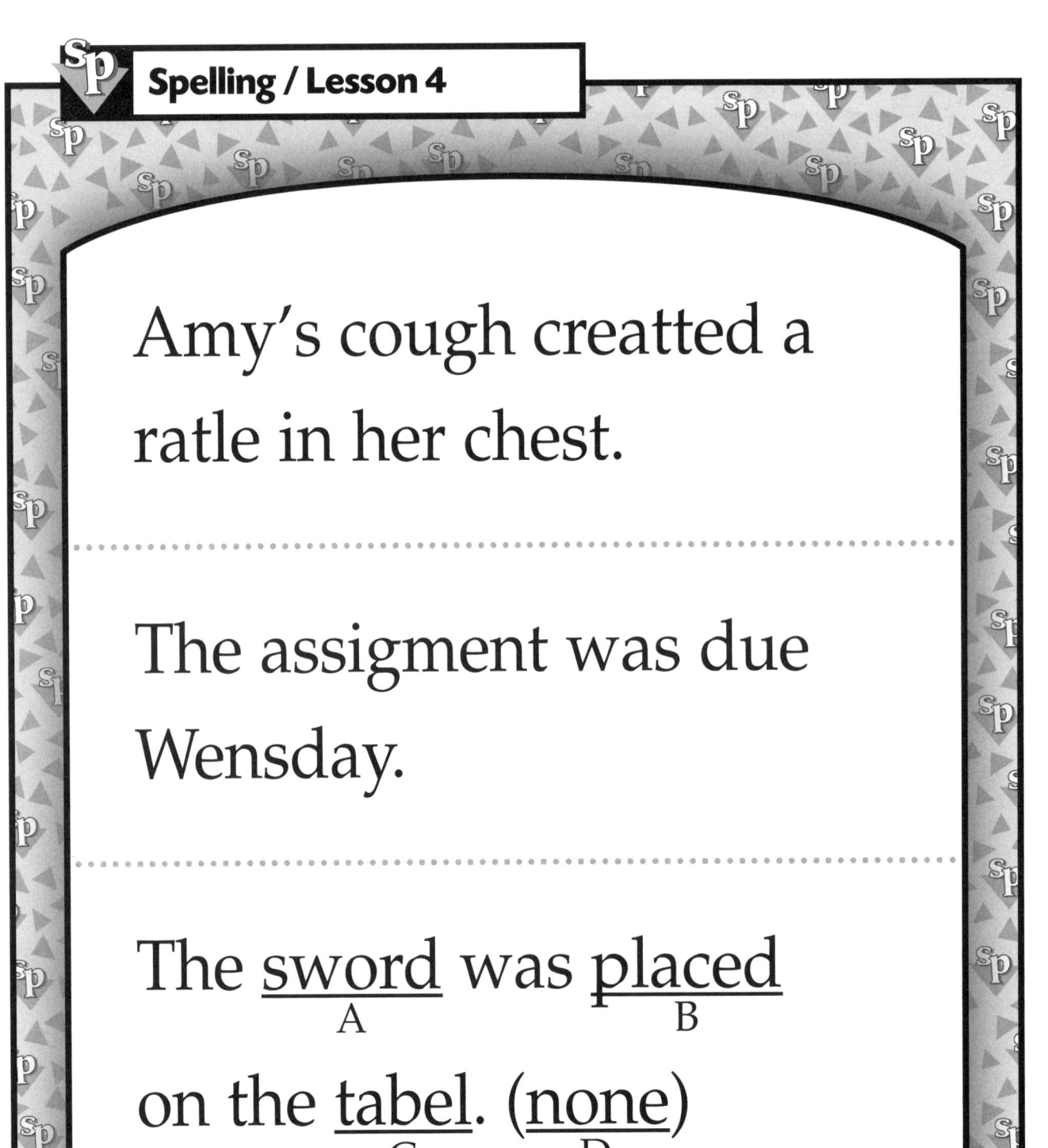

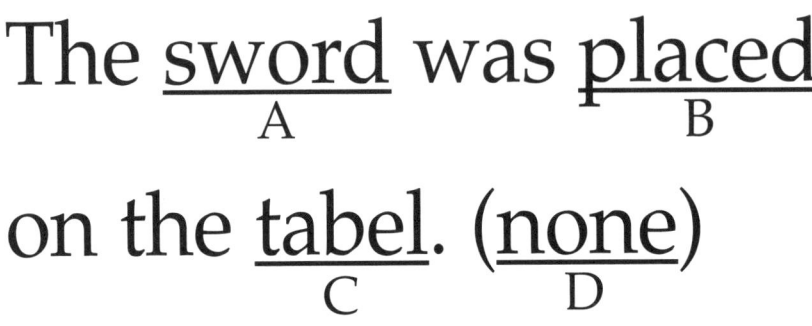

Amy's cough creatted a ratle in her chest.

The assigment was due Wensday.

The <u>sword</u> was <u>placed</u>
     A   B

on the <u>tabel</u>. (<u>none</u>)
       C   D

☐ A   ☐ B   ☐ C   ☐ D

Spelling / Lesson 5

The class will usualy find all the mistaks.

The studnets were sincerely sorry.

Martin's <u>stories</u> were
        A

<u>quiet</u> <u>believable</u>. (<u>none</u>)
  B   C   D

☐ A   ☐ B   ☐ C   ☐ D

Spelling / Lesson 6

Rover groweled at the poeple lined on the street.

He dosn't clean his room on Tusday.

Juan had truble with the
　　　A　　B

loose change.　(none)
　C　　　　　　　　D

☐ A　☐ B　☐ C　☐ D

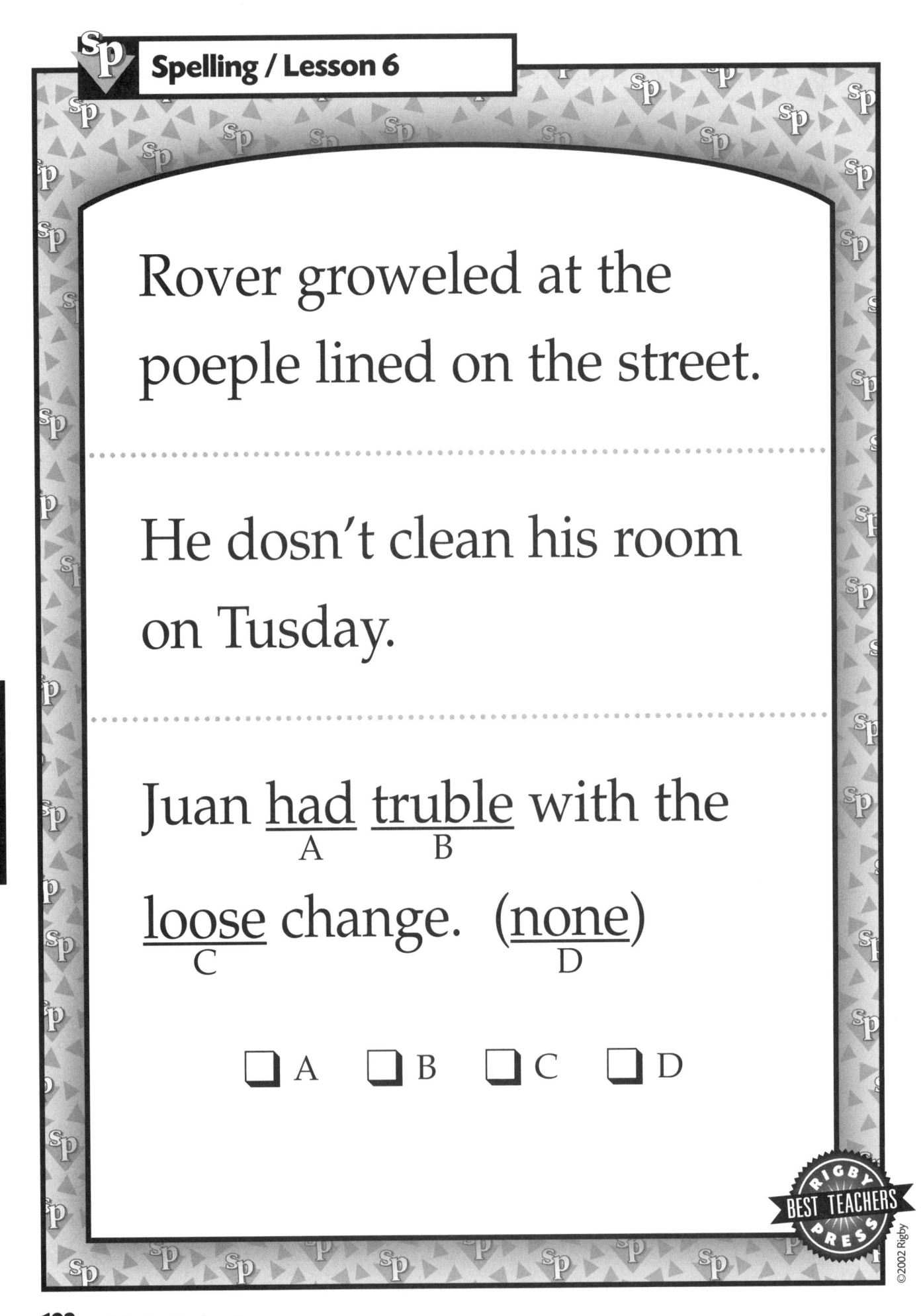

Spelling / Lesson 7

They'er haveing dificulty with arthematic.

Sevral girls were exsited about the Febuary party.

Jordan woudn't help decorate the gymnasium.
       A   B   C
(none)
 D

☐ A ☐ B ☐ C ☐ D

Ready, Set, Edit

Spelling / Lesson 8

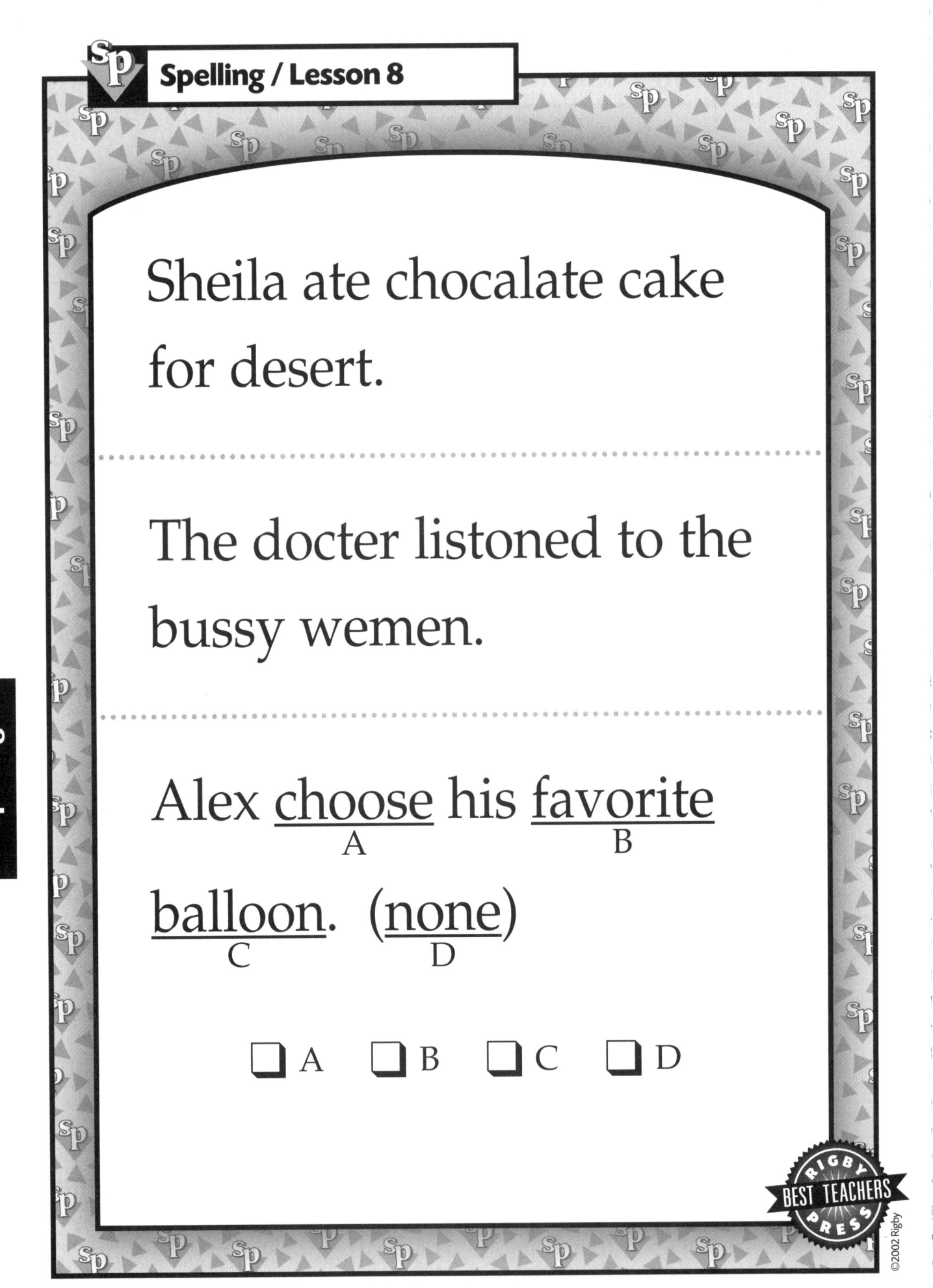

Sheila ate chocalate cake for desert.

The docter listoned to the bussy wemen.

Alex <u>choose</u> his <u>favorite</u>
　　　 A　　　　　 B
<u>balloon</u>. (<u>none</u>)
　C　　　　　D

☐ A　☐ B　☐ C　☐ D

Spelling / Lesson 9

Suzanne was amased by the hieght of the building.

Sean was makeing his faverite chocalate cookies.

Chris <u>went</u> <u>straght</u> to the <u>classroom</u>. (<u>none</u>)
    A   B   C   D

☐ A ☐ B ☐ C ☐ D

Spelling / Lesson 10

The teachar allways wears preety shoes.

The class was writing leters to friends.

Juan <u>offen</u> <u>plays</u> with other <u>friends</u>. (<u>none</u>)
     A   B   C   D

☐ A   ☐ B   ☐ C   ☐ D

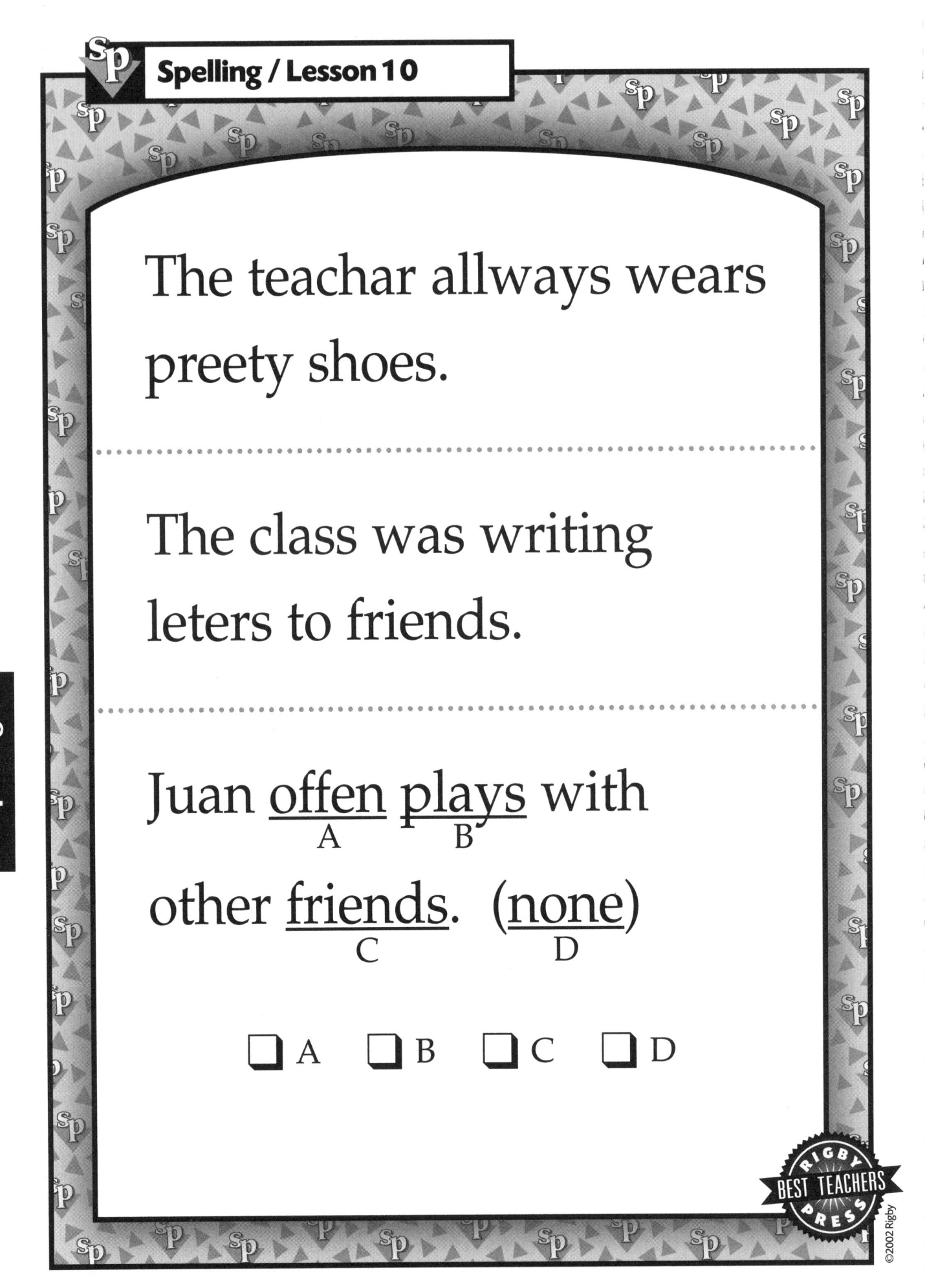

Spelling / Lesson 11

Tommorrow the studnets will practise for the game.

Bob enjoyes travelling during summer vacation.

This <u>was</u> <u>their</u> <u>frist</u> band concert. (<u>none</u>)
　　　A　　B　　C　　　　　　　D

☐ A ☐ B ☐ C ☐ D

Spelling / Lesson 12

Laura could't find Rout 7 on the map.

Justin plays out side alot on Saterday.

He dosn't want a bike for
   A   B
his birthday. (none)
     C   D

☐ A   ☐ B   ☐ C   ☐ D

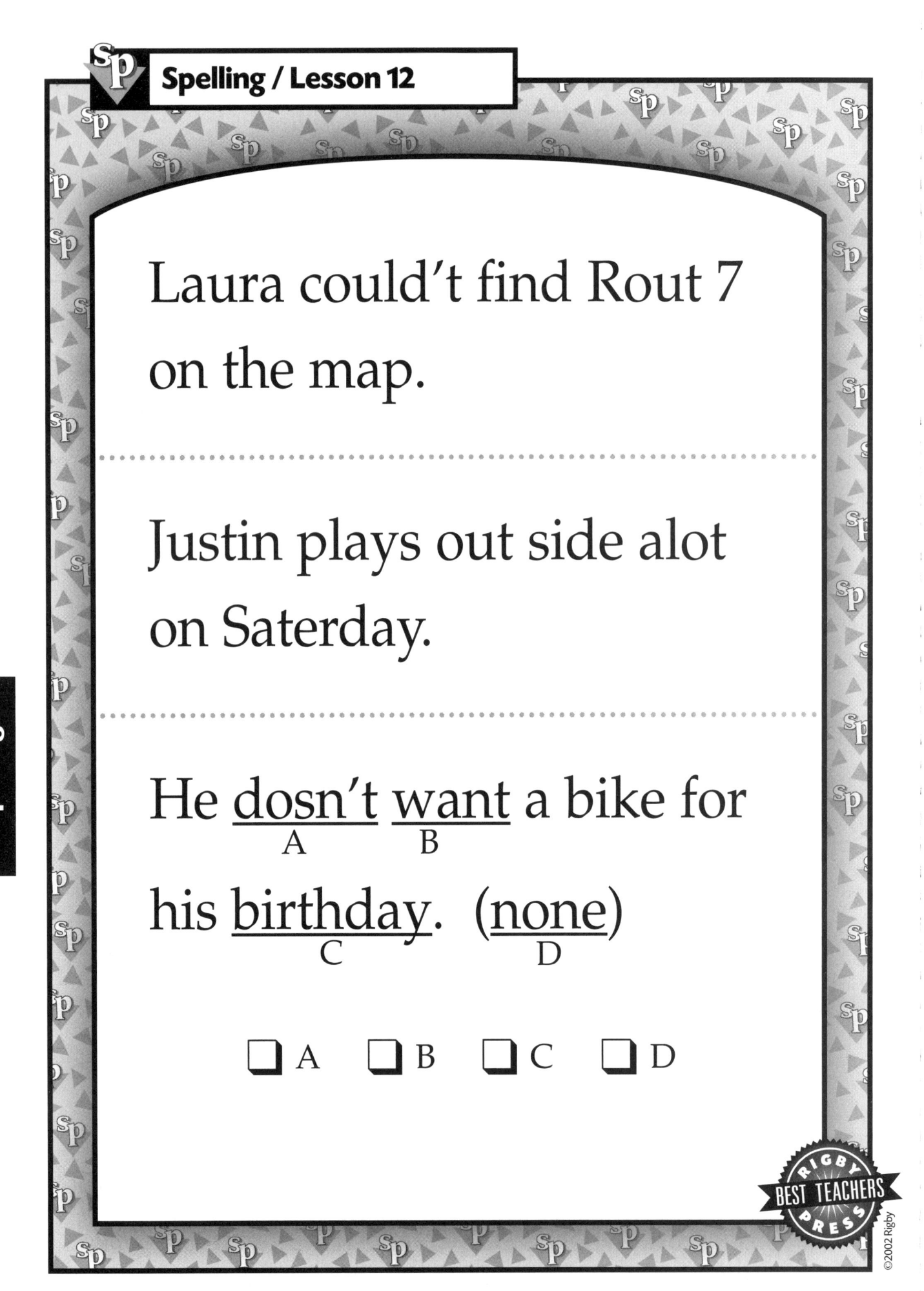

Spelling / Lesson 13

The sckool bell will ring at any minite.

- -

Nether boy would practise befor the game.

- -

Tom is <u>having</u> <u>surgery</u> at
          A   B
the <u>hospitol</u>. (<u>none</u>)
    C   D

❏ A ❏ B ❏ C ❏ D

Spelling / Lesson 14

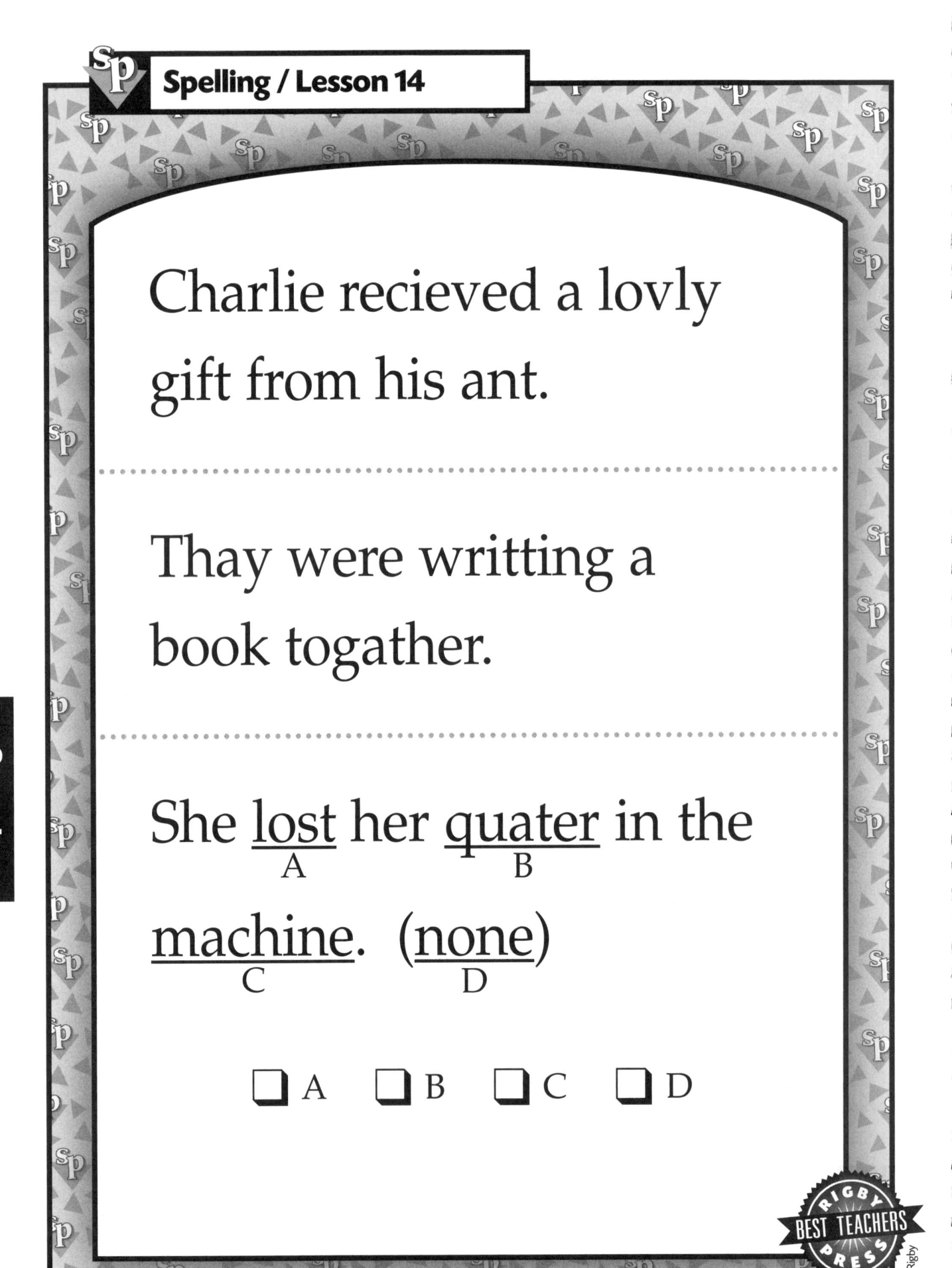

Charlie recieved a lovly gift from his ant.

Thay were writting a book togather.

She lost her quater in the
     A   B
machine. (none)
   C   D

☐ A   ☐ B   ☐ C   ☐ D

Spelling / Lesson 15

Rich wanted a thrid peice of cake.

The whit shose were left out side.

<u>Somthing</u> was <u>wrong</u>
    A   B

with the new <u>candle</u>.
                           C

(<u>none</u>)
  D

☐ A   ☐ B   ☐ C   ☐ D

Spelling / Lesson 16

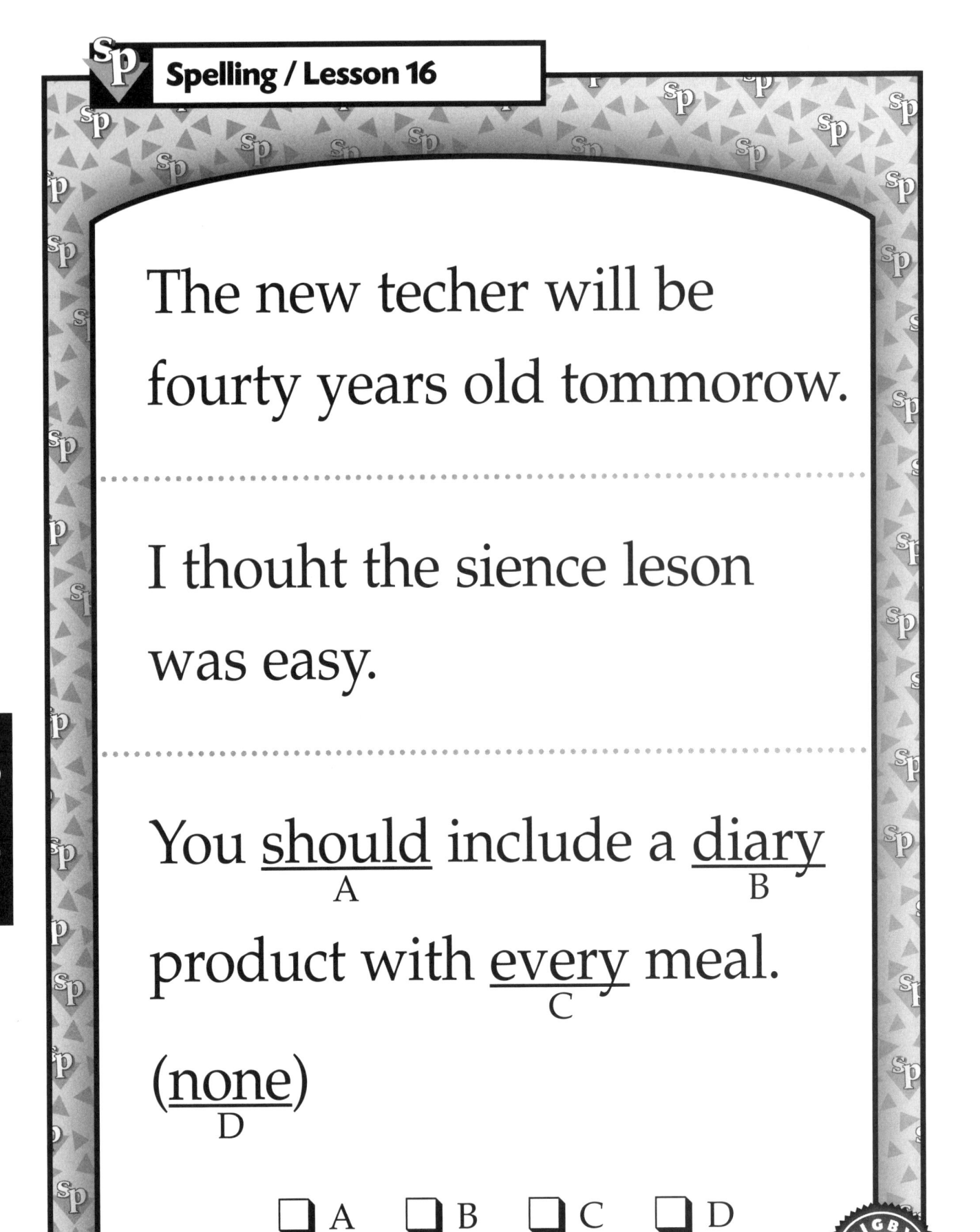

The new techer will be fourty years old tommorow.

I thouht the sience leson was easy.

You <u>should</u> include a <u>diary</u>
     A   B
product with <u>every</u> meal.
                      C
(<u>none</u>)
  D

☐ A   ☐ B   ☐ C   ☐ D

Spelling / Lesson 17

Russell went straght to the stoer to by suger for his mothor.

The class biult a playground for evryone.

John is <u>studing</u> for his
      A

<u>geography</u> <u>test</u>. (<u>none</u>)
     B   C   D

☐ A ☐ B ☐ C ☐ D

Spelling / Lesson 18

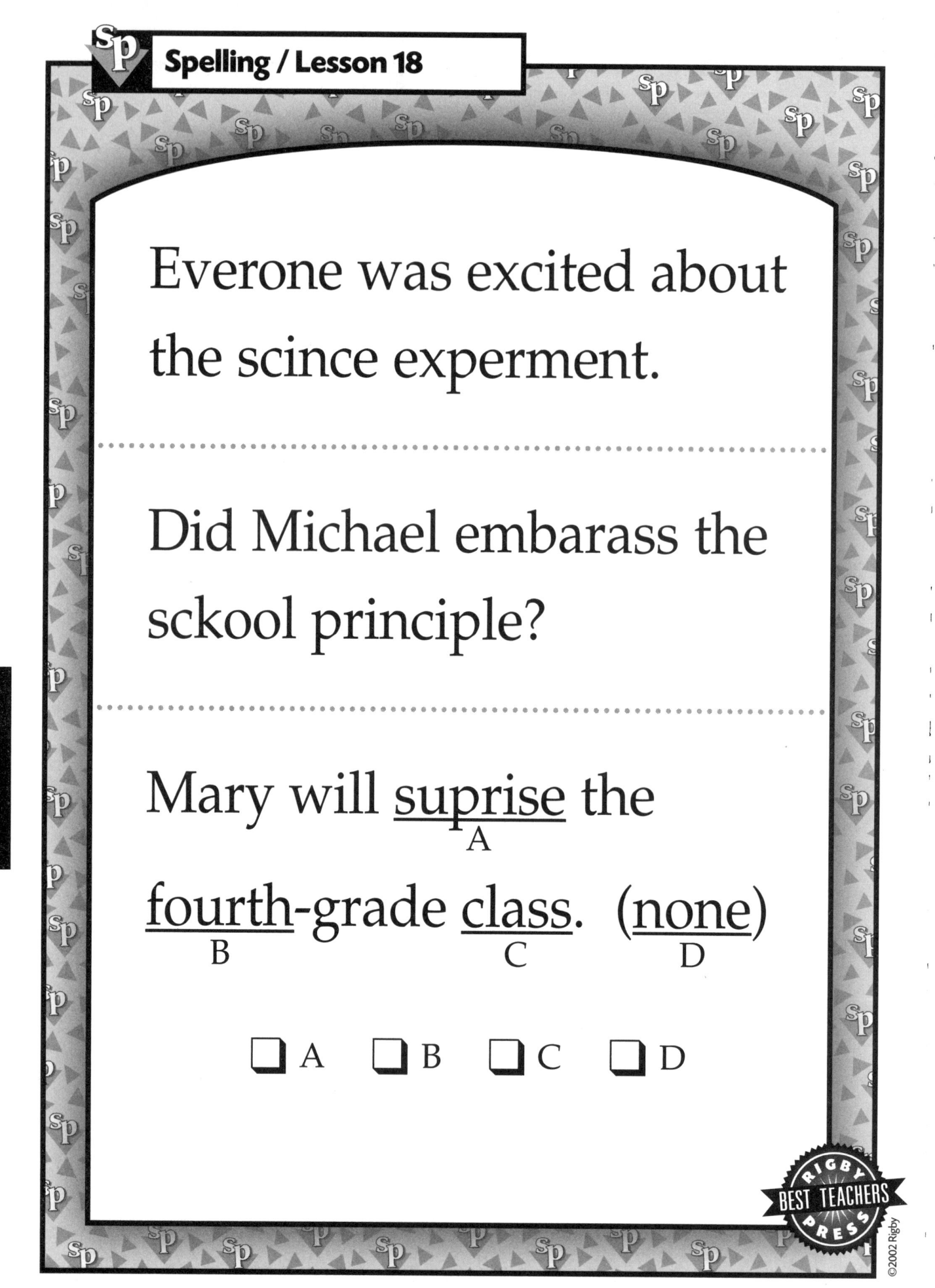

Everone was excited about the scince experment.

Did Michael embarass the sckool principle?

Mary will <u>suprise</u> the
          A

<u>fourth-grade</u> <u>class</u>. (<u>none</u>)
      B   C   D

☐ A   ☐ B   ☐ C   ☐ D

Spelling / Lesson 19

The class should not interupt the principle.

Is forth grade similiar to fifth grade?

The new teacher is plesant
       A   B
and interesting. (none)
       C   D

❏ A ❏ B ❏ C ❏ D

Spelling / Lesson 20

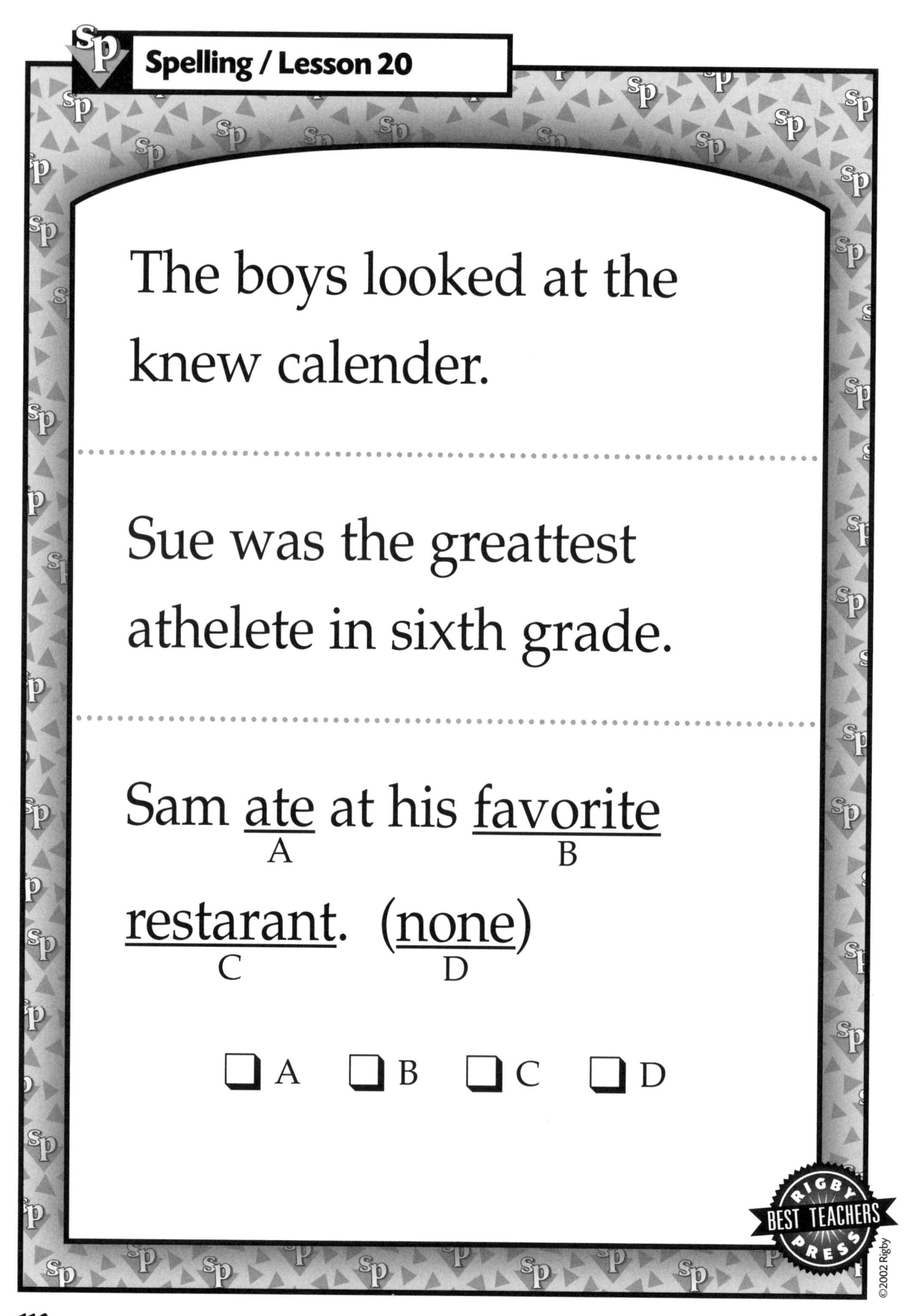

The boys looked at the knew calender.

....

Sue was the greattest athelete in sixth grade.

....

Sam <u>ate</u> at his <u>favorite</u>
     A   B

<u>restarant</u>. (<u>none</u>)
 C   D

❑ A   ❑ B   ❑ C   ❑ D

Spelling / Lesson 21

The studnets payed for the rythm instrumnts.

Josh requested a reciept from the clerk.

<u>Its</u> a <u>valuable</u> <u>bracelet</u>.
 A   B   C
(<u>none</u>)
  D

☐ A   ☐ B   ☐ C   ☐ D

Spelling / Lesson 22

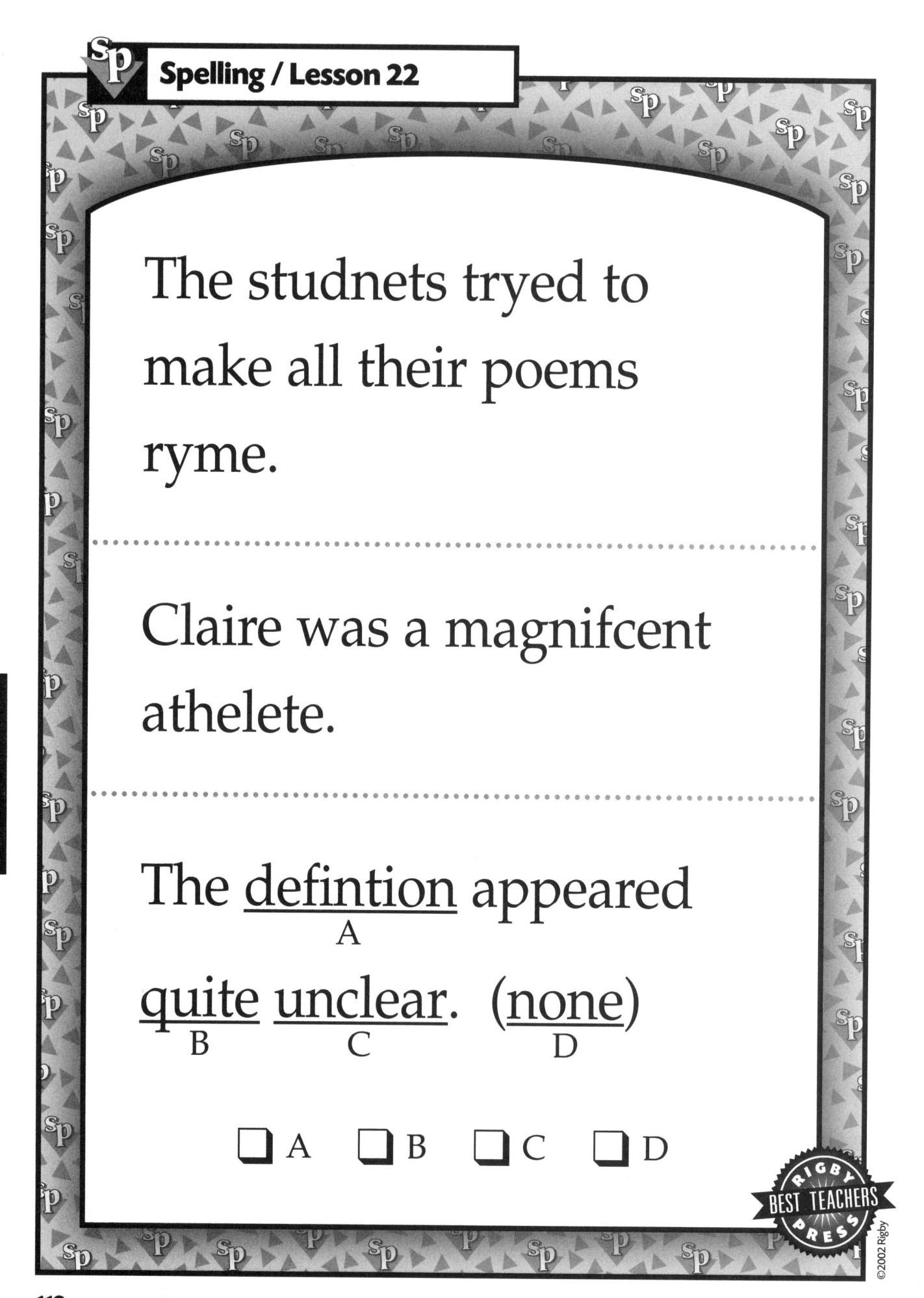

The studnets tryed to make all their poems ryme.

Claire was a magnifcent athelete.

The defintion appeared
    A
quite unclear. (none)
  B   C   D

☐ A   ☐ B   ☐ C   ☐ D

Spelling / Lesson 23

The performance was insparational.

The errers on the mathmatics test were too numorous.

Mr. Shore's <u>neice</u> was a
           A
<u>quiet</u> <u>student</u>. (<u>none</u>)
  B   C   D

☐ A ☐ B ☐ C ☐ D

Spelling / Lesson 24

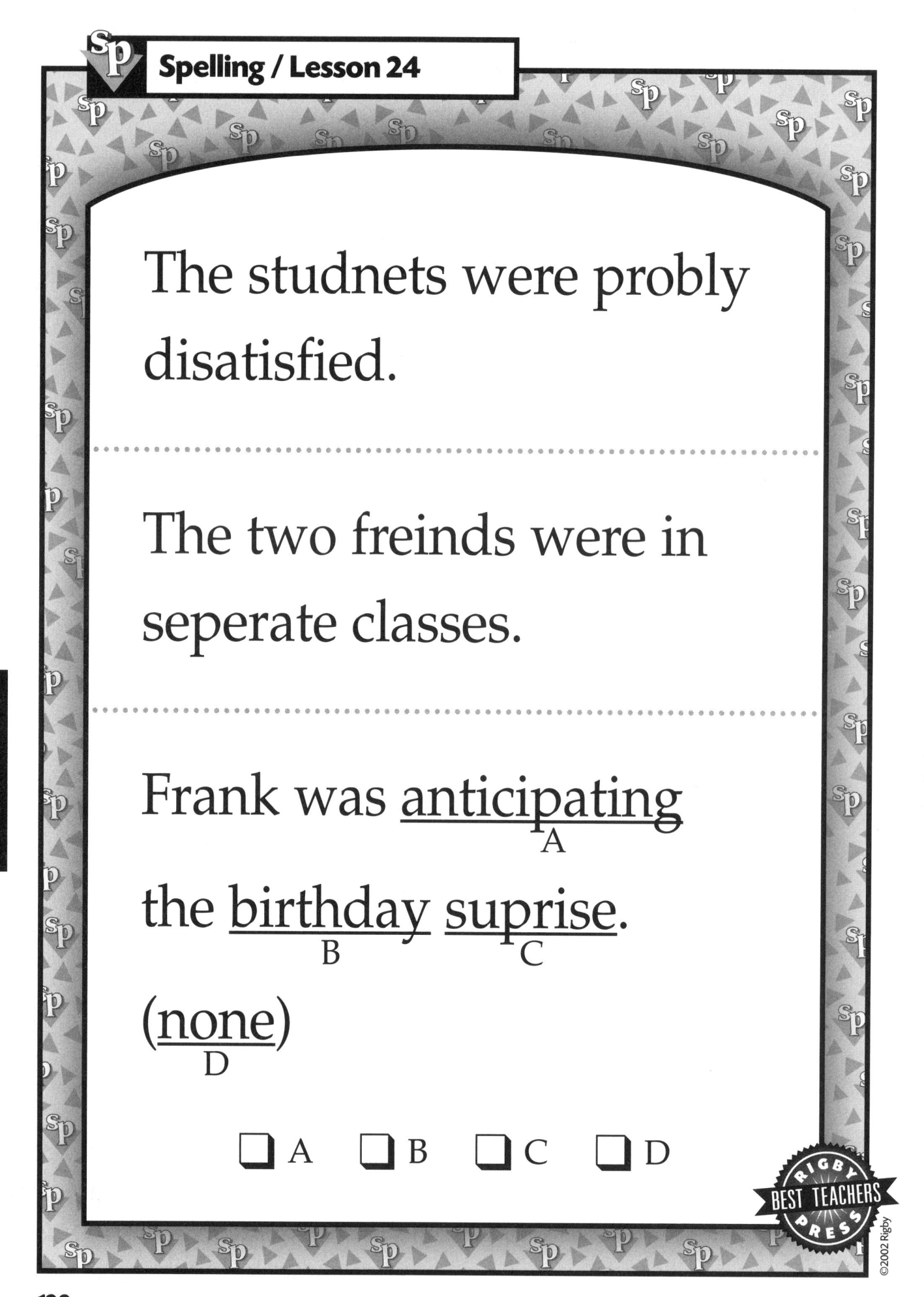

The studnets were probly disatisfied.

The two freinds were in seperate classes.

Frank was <u>anticipating</u> the <u>birthday</u> <u>suprise</u>.
            A   B   C
(<u>none</u>)
 D

☐ A   ☐ B   ☐ C   ☐ D

Spelling / Lesson 25

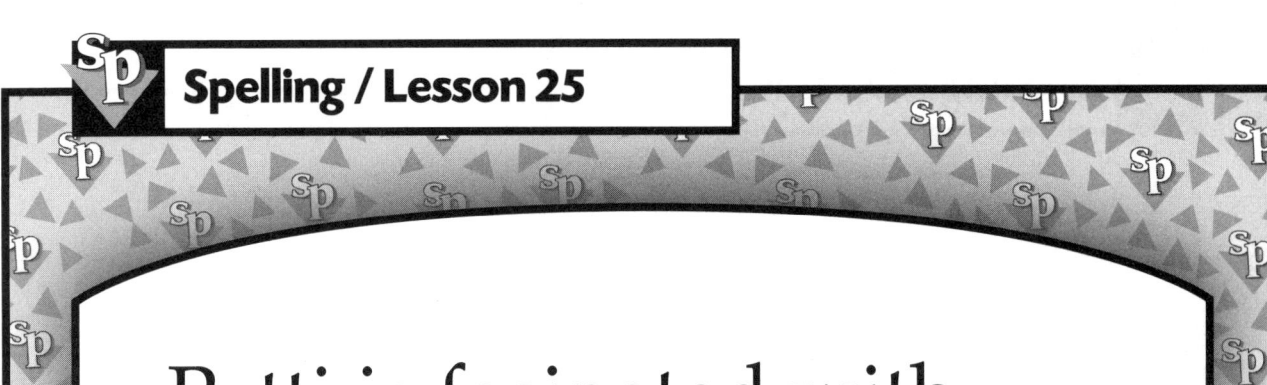

Patti is fasinated with mystery novals.

It never ocurred to the feriends to clean the asle.

The <u>exercise</u> class was
     A

<u>probably</u> <u>disastrous</u>.
  B   C

(<u>none</u>)
  D

☐ A   ☐ B   ☐ C   ☐ D

Ready, Set, Edit

Spelling / Lesson 26

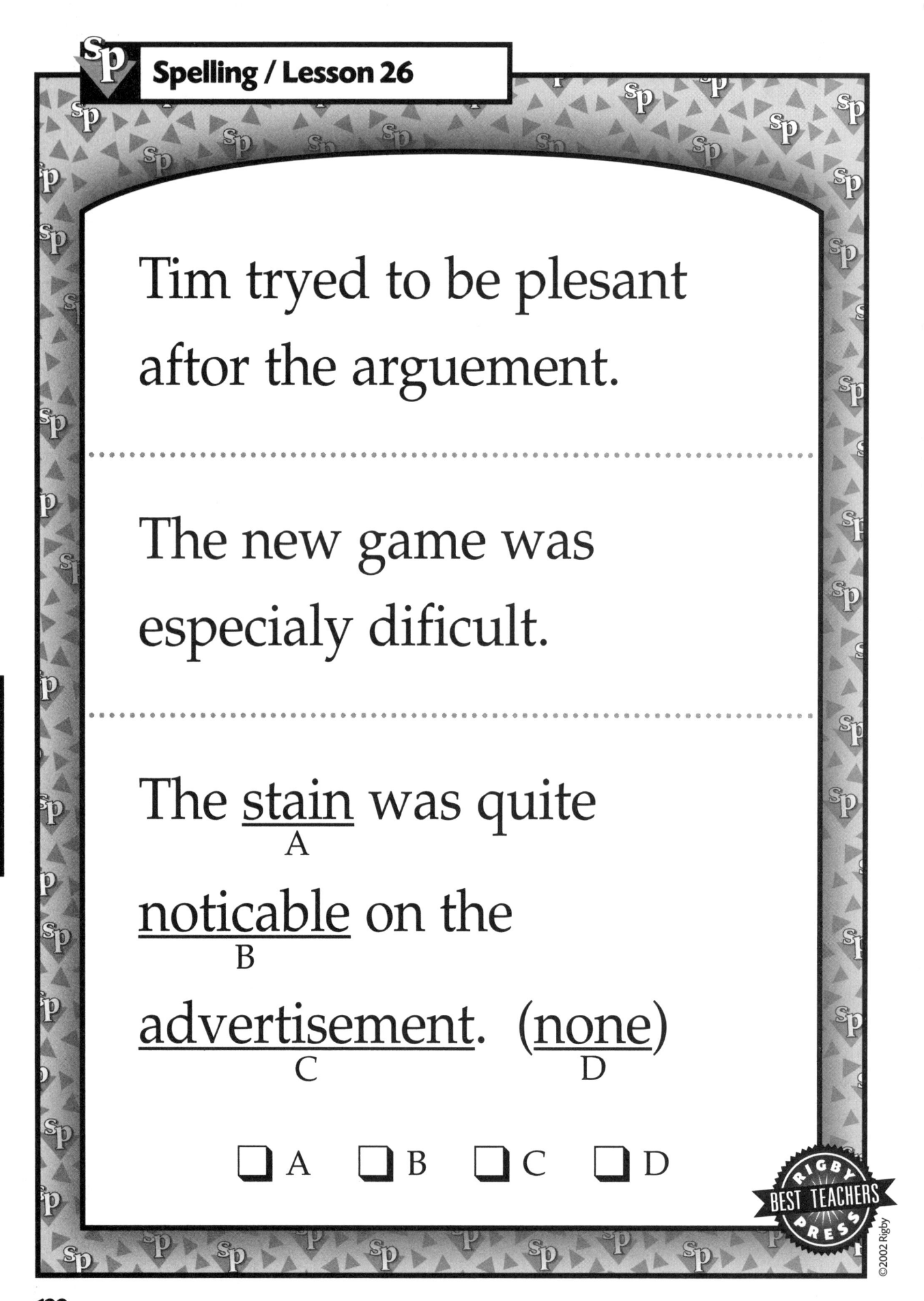

Tim tryed to be plesant aftor the arguement.

The new game was especialy dificult.

The <u>stain</u> was quite
     A
<u>noticable</u> on the
     B
<u>advertisement</u>. (<u>none</u>)
     C   D

☐ A ☐ B ☐ C ☐ D

Spelling / Lesson 27

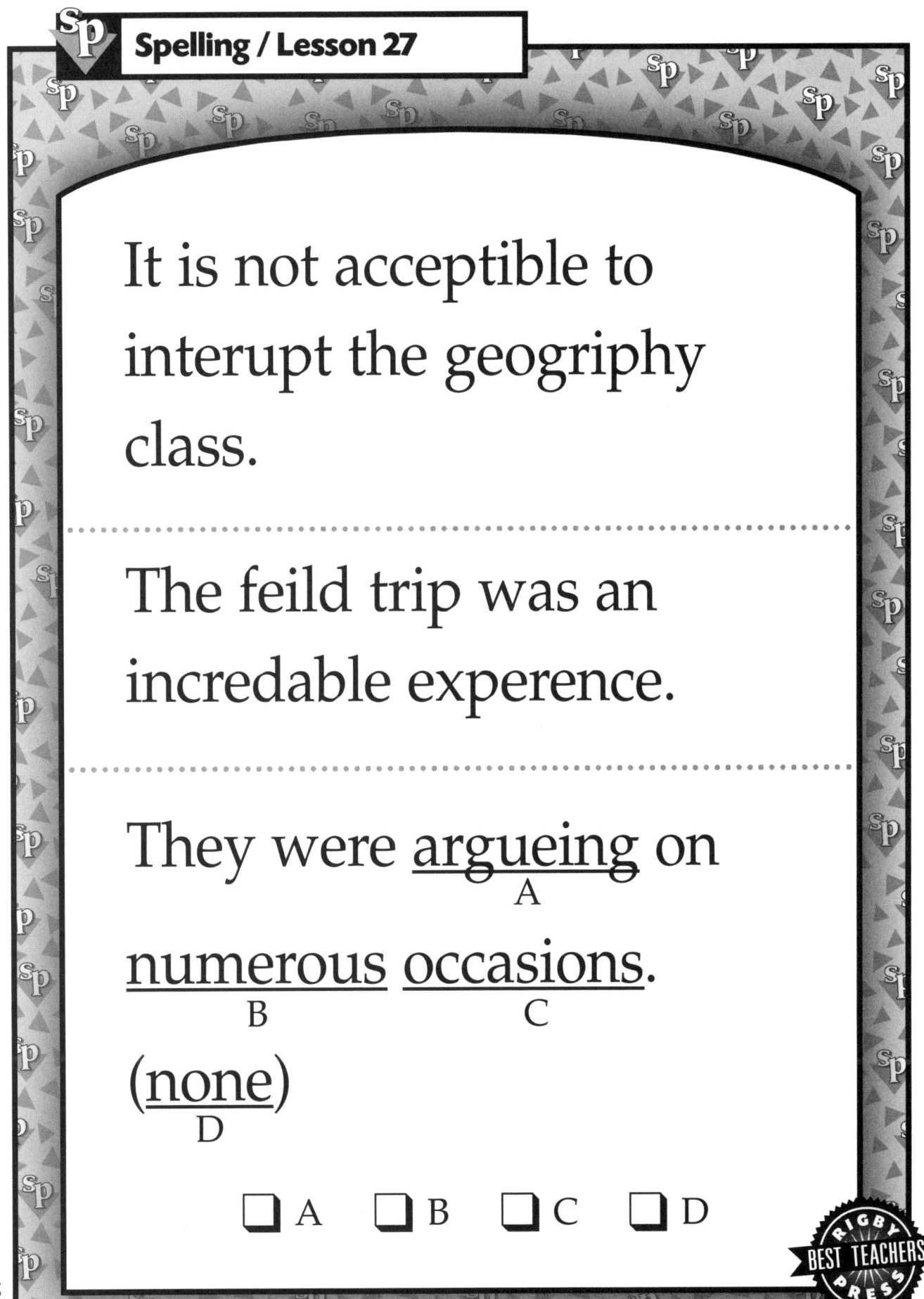

It is not acceptible to interupt the geogriphy class.

The feild trip was an incredable experence.

They were <u>argueing</u> on
       A
<u>numerous</u> <u>occasions</u>.
    B   C
(<u>none</u>)
  D

☐ A   ☐ B   ☐ C   ☐ D

Spelling / Lesson 28

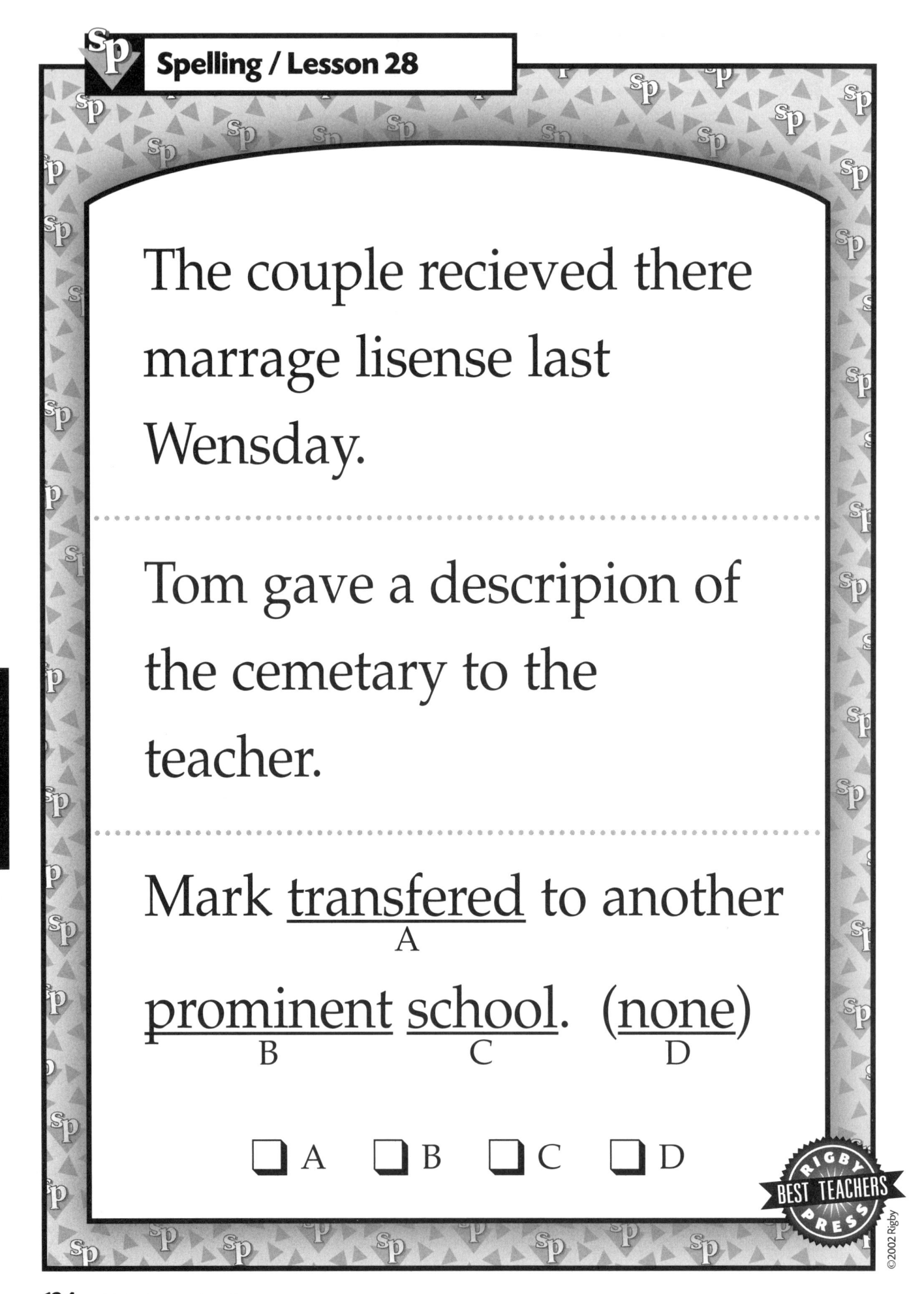

The couple recieved there marrage lisense last Wensday.

Tom gave a descripion of the cemetary to the teacher.

Mark <u>transfered</u> to another <u>prominent</u> <u>school</u>. <u>(none)</u>
       A   B   C   D

☐ A   ☐ B   ☐ C   ☐ D

Spelling / Lesson 29

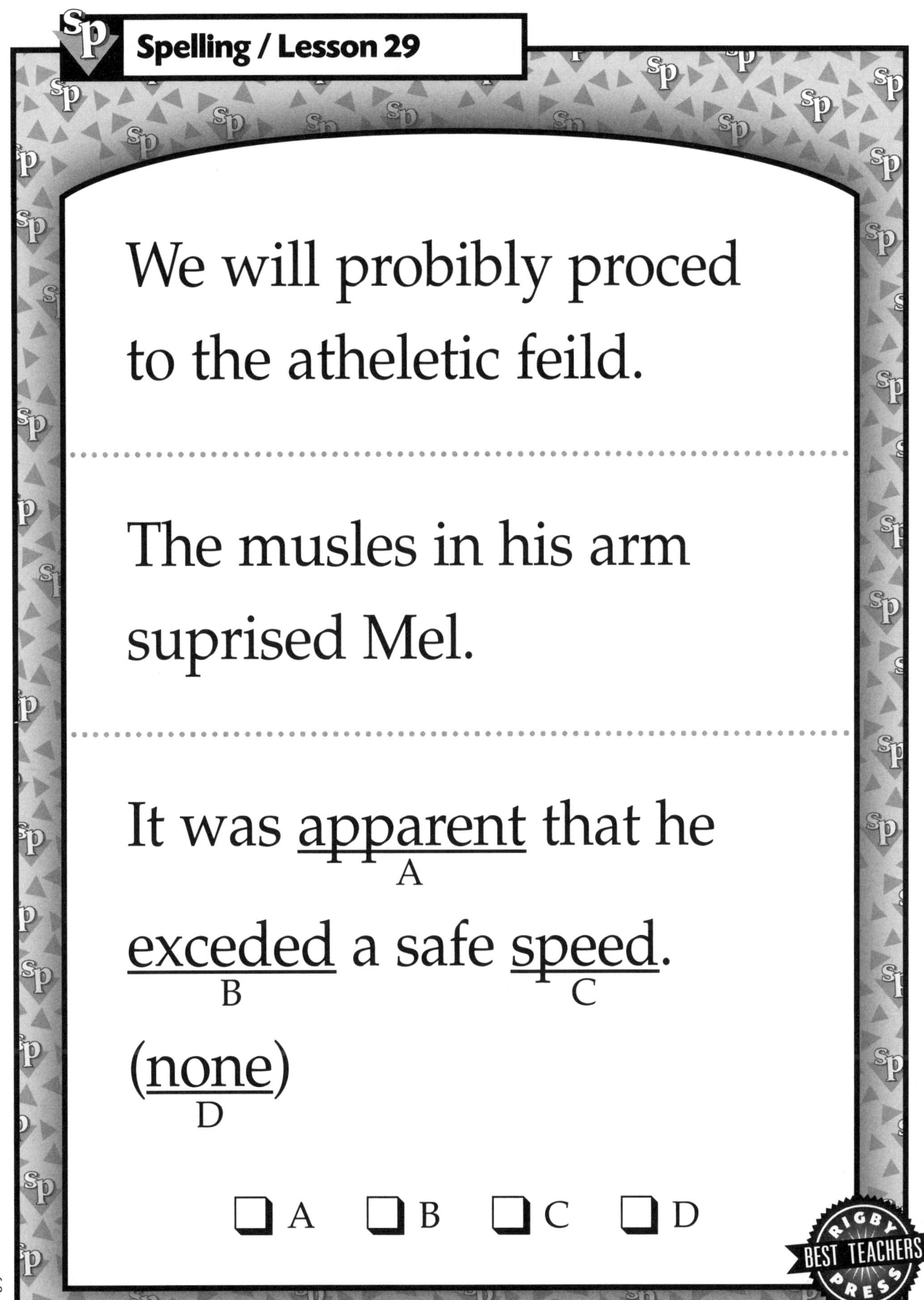

We will probibly proced to the atheletic feild.

The musles in his arm suprised Mel.

It was <u>apparent</u> that he
         A
<u>exceded</u> a safe <u>speed</u>.
   B   C
(<u>none</u>)
   D

❏ A ❏ B ❏ C ❏ D

Spelling / Lesson 30

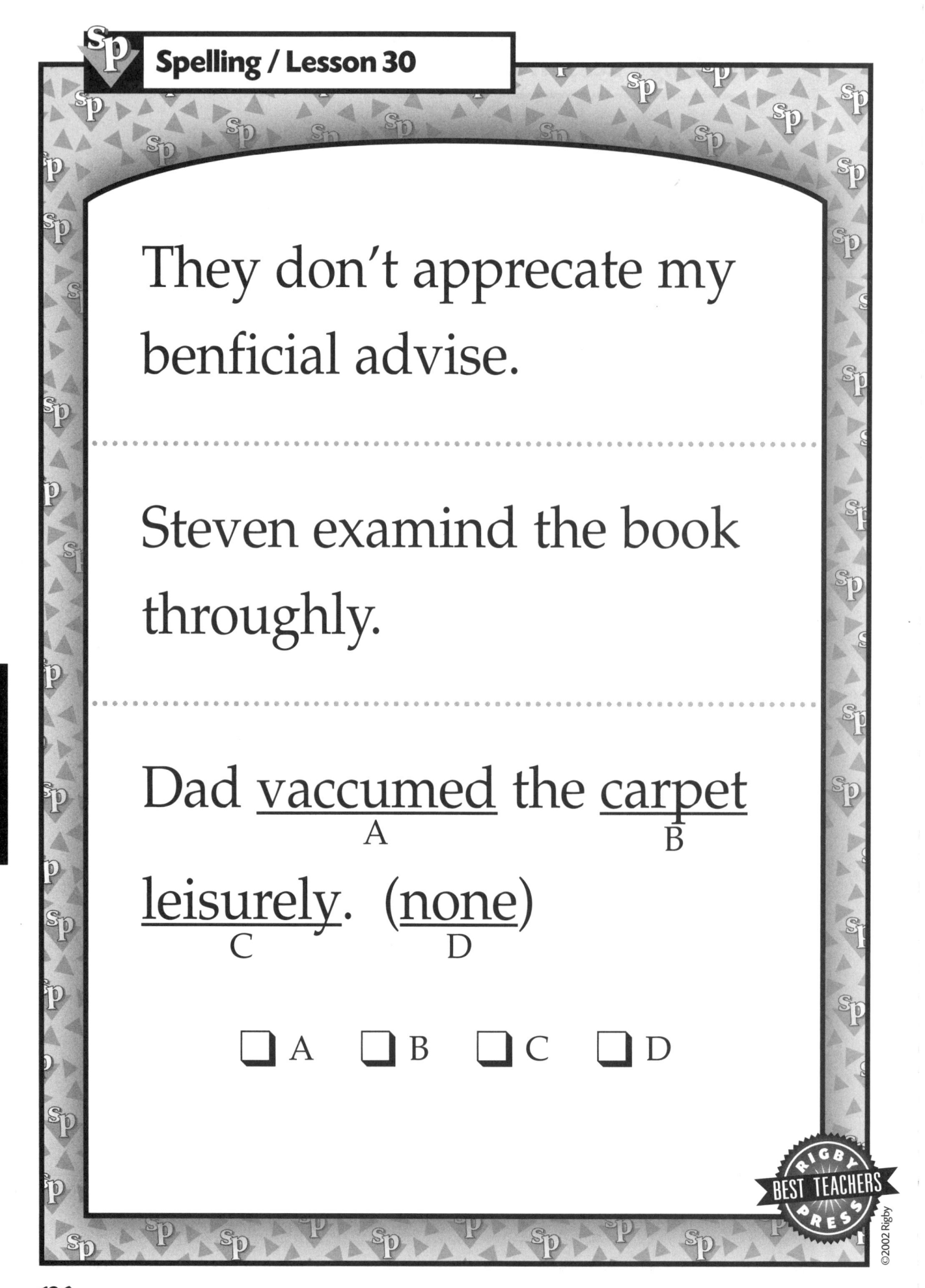

They don't apprecate my benficial advise.

Steven examind the book throughly.

Dad <u>vaccumed</u> the <u>carpet</u>
     A   B

<u>leisurely</u>. (<u>none</u>)
   C   D

☐ A   ☐ B   ☐ C   ☐ D

Variety / Lesson 1

sue lamb poped the video into the vcr.

last night we watched a tv program about mount rushmore said henry

"<u>Have</u> you ever seen the
  A
<u>washington</u> <u>Monument</u>?"
    B   C
asked Sam. (<u>none</u>)
              D

☐ A   ☐ B   ☐ C   ☐ D

Variety / Lesson 2

studnets have allways needed to talk eat sleep and play.

now in order to play today you must complet you're work.

You see, the food is quiet hot. (none)
A   B   C   D

☐ A   ☐ B   ☐ C   ☐ D

Variety / Lesson 3

while your their check out the english book

after lunch its time to study the constitution

President Kennedy <u>lived</u>_A in the <u>White</u>_B <u>house</u>_C. (<u>none</u>)_D

☐ A ☐ B ☐ C ☐ D

Variety / Lesson 4

if you no what you want, luke says, you will get it

---

soon his frends will start to laugh

<u>Beleiving</u> in yourself will
    A

make <u>your</u> life more
      B

<u>enjoyable</u>. (<u>none</u>)
  C   D

☐ A   ☐ B   ☐ C   ☐ D

Variety / Lesson 5

i want to be their to fix any thing that gose rong

john realy likes chating on the telefone

JoJo Publishing <u>company</u>
                    A
may soon <u>close</u> <u>its</u> doors.
           B   C
(<u>none</u>)
  D

☐ A ☐ B ☐ C ☐ D

Variety / Lesson 6

president clinton he visited china

their best friends connie and samantha ate at goldmans restaurant.

Greg <u>has took</u> his <u>book to</u> the <u>cafeteria</u>. <u>(none)</u>
　　　　A　　　　　　B　　　　C　　　　D

☐ A　☐ B　☐ C　☐ D

Variety / Lesson 7

me and my friend doesn't like to visit the Docter

did you remind kevin about jennifers birthday on monday april 7th

<u>Yes</u> Colleen <u>and I</u> love eating <u>chocolate</u>! <u>(none)</u>
  A   B   C   D

❏ A   ❏ B   ❏ C   ❏ D

Variety / Lesson 8

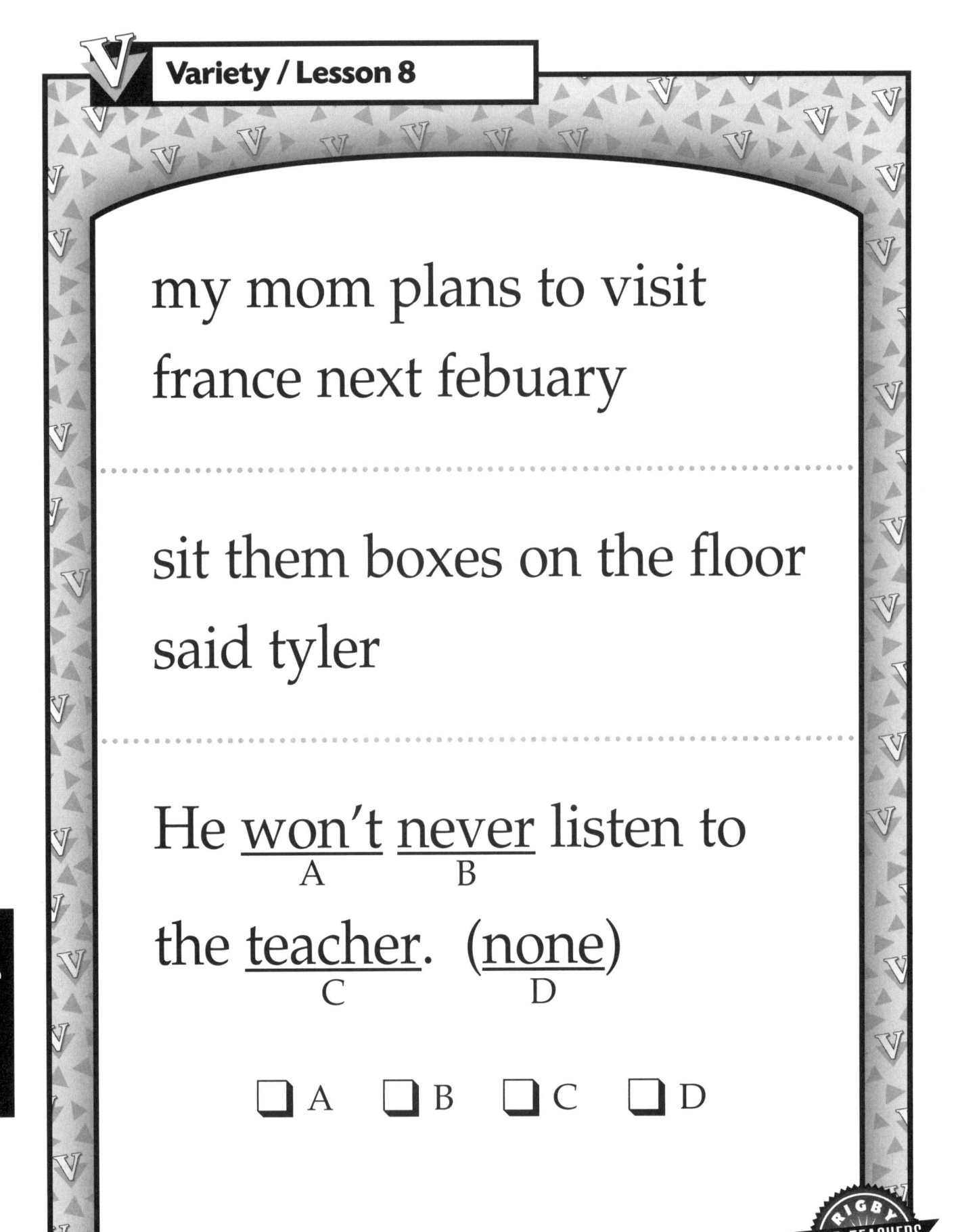

my mom plans to visit france next febuary

sit them boxes on the floor said tyler

He won't never listen to
    A   B

the teacher. (none)
    C   D

☐ A   ☐ B   ☐ C   ☐ D

Variety / Lesson 9

no my dog want play at fairmont park

my brother and me has took the books to school

Julie and <u>Mom</u> watched
         A
the <u>Game</u> on <u>TV</u>. (<u>none</u>)
    B   C   D

☐ A   ☐ B   ☐ C   ☐ D

Variety / Lesson 10

i hope tonyas mom doesnt break nothing said jimmy

---

the school chorus sang america the beautiful

Jasmine and <u>me</u> <u>don't</u> want <u>any</u>. (<u>none</u>)
         A   B   C   D

☐ A ☐ B ☐ C ☐ D

Variety / Lesson 11

janes mom buyed a new book called time for baking

the childrn didn't no it were president washingtons birthday

The <u>too</u> boys <u>sang</u> "Moon River" with zest. (<u>none</u>)
   A   B   C   D

❑ A   ❑ B   ❑ C   ❑ D

Ready, Set, Edit

Variety / Lesson 12

tell mrs kimball you're new teacher the Schools schedule

her mom said lets eat at daves dinor

He <u>don't</u> <u>know</u> the <u>answer</u>
     A   B   C

to the problem. (<u>none</u>)
                             D

☐ A   ☐ B   ☐ C   ☐ D

Variety / Lesson 13

Judy and me has ate all the candy therefore we will have none left for the party

put on you're coat said mom and you're gloves

Scott and <u>I</u> are going to
         A
visit <u>Aunt</u> Martha next
      B
<u>Thursday</u>. (<u>none</u>)
   C   D

❑ A   ❑ B   ❑ C   ❑ D

Variety / Lesson 14

have you saw fido my cat

the too girls wants to play at kims house

John's report is more better
　A　　　　　　　　B

than Mary's report.
　　　　C

(none)
　D

☐ A　☐ B　☐ C　☐ D

Variety / Lesson 15

sam ain't got transportation to brookfield park

did you thank principal johnson for the books pencils and computers

Mrs. Tesh <u>teached</u> the
            A
<u>students</u> <u>geometry</u>. (<u>none</u>)
   B   C   D

❏ A ❏ B ❏ C ❏ D

Variety / Lesson 16

my dad throwed a ball to
jordan and i

them books belong hear
on miss tylers desk

Mrs. Porter's class
       —————
         A
explored the west last
                ————
                  B
spring. (none)
——————   ————
   C   D

❏ A   ❏ B   ❏ C   ❏ D

Variety / Lesson 17

did you find this here book at the store

Melissa and me shopped at southside department store last thrusday

Put <u>them</u> books in your desk now. (none)
    A   B   C   D

☐ A   ☐ B   ☐ C   ☐ D

Variety / Lesson 18

ricardo and me didn't find no broken bikes at joeys house

---

pete must set quiet in dr blacks office

Her mom <u>asked</u>,
     A
"<u>Would</u> you like to visit
  B
<u>State Park</u>?" (<u>none</u>)
    C   D

☐ A ☐ B ☐ C ☐ D

Variety / Lesson 19

The howe family moved to thirty second avenue charlotte north carolina last july

no he don't belong hear

He had gave the ball to
     A

his mom. (none)
B C   D

☐ A   ☐ B   ☐ C   ☐ D

Variety / Lesson 20

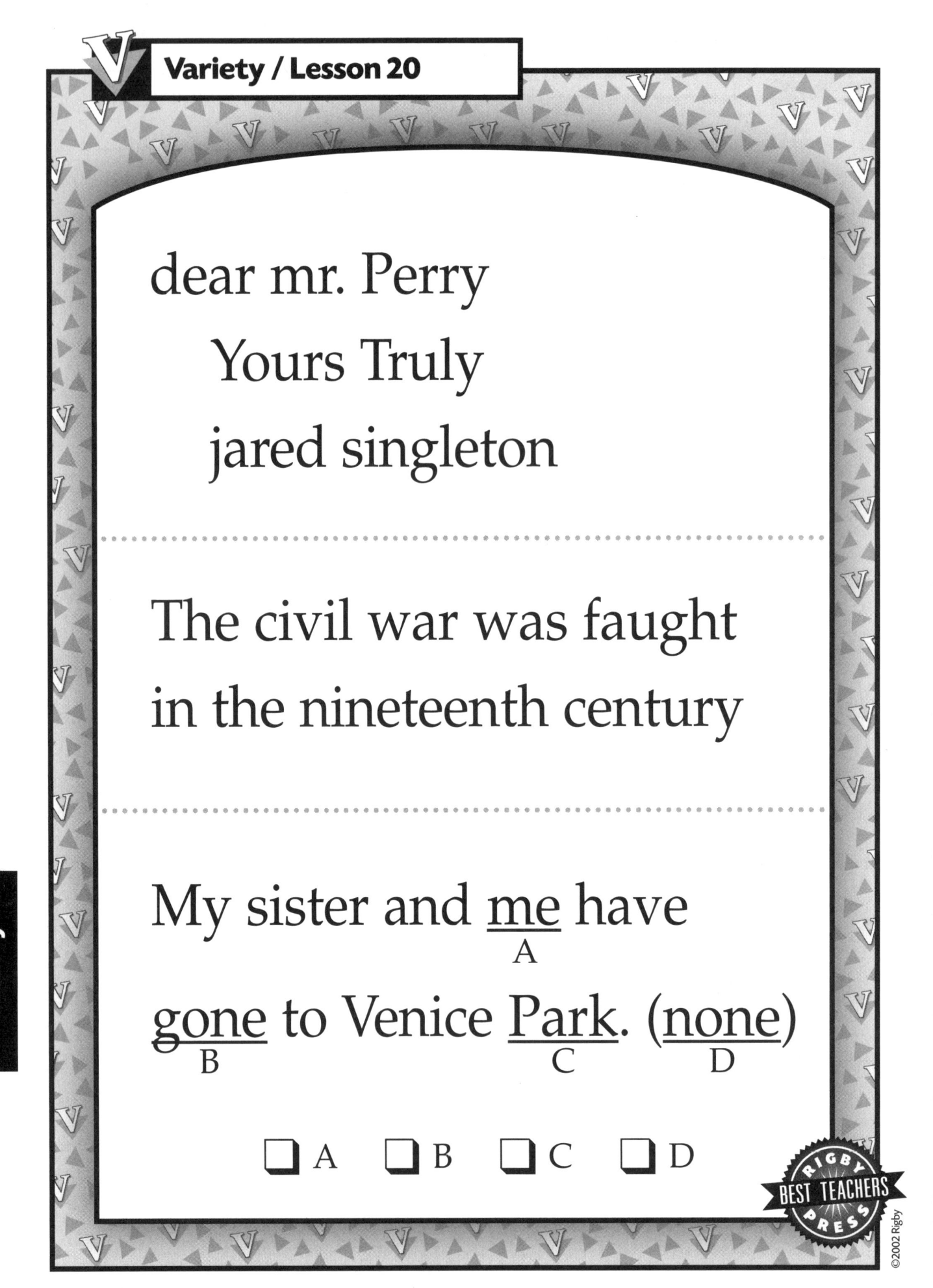

dear mr. Perry

Yours Truly

jared singleton

The civil war was faught in the nineteenth century

My sister and <u>me</u> have
          A

<u>gone</u> to Venice <u>Park</u>. (<u>none</u>)
 B   C   D

☐ A ☐ B ☐ C ☐ D

Variety / Lesson 21

greg and me would of gone their but we was tired

sue and her Mom celebrated at the Restaurant on pine street

Chuck and I didn't want none. (none)
　　　　　A　　B　　　　　C　　　D

☐ A　☐ B　☐ C　☐ D

Variety / Lesson 22

there class left on may 3 2001 to go to banter park

Jane and me has ate all the cookys

I often read "The Boa
         ―――
           A
Constrictor," a poem, to
―――――――   ――
    B   C
my little brother. (none)
                     ――――
                       D

☐ A ☐ B ☐ C ☐ D

Variety / Lesson 23

paul is more young than his brother therefore he goes to a different school

annie you should have give you're books to juan said mom

The <u>boys</u> <u>have went</u> to <u>Angela's</u> house. (<u>none</u>)
　　　A　　　B　　　　　C　　　　　　D

☐ A ☐ B ☐ C ☐ D

Variety / Lesson 24

mom said joe these shoes don't fit you're feet no more

eduardo your planning I know to study hard for the test

John's pencils was broken. (none)
　A　　　　　B　　C　　　D

☐ A　☐ B　☐ C　☐ D

Variety / Lesson 25

tom and him had ate before mom arrived

....

if you misbehave you will not be allowed to visit east park

....

The game <u>will be played</u> at Easton Middle <u>school</u> next <u>Wednesday</u>. (<u>none</u>)
             A   B   C   D

❏ A   ❏ B   ❏ C   ❏ D

Variety / Lesson 26

maria read an excellent Book about australia written buy jake venn

tom by bread milk and sugar at east market said dad

The <u>children</u> <u>had written</u> letters to Dan and <u>I</u>.
　　A　　　　B　　　　　　　　　　C

(<u>none</u>)
　D

☐ A   ☐ B   ☐ C   ☐ D

Variety / Lesson 27

class please set quietly and listen to mr garvey and i

mark he studied his spelling completed his math and read the novel, the tower of terror

"Have you completed your work, Tom?" (none)
　　　　　　　A　　　B　　　C　　　D

❑ A　❑ B　❑ C　❑ D

Variety / Lesson 28

did you read the article called fire in the city in last weeks times magazine

ruth she don't eat her vegetables drink her milk or clean her tray

The children <u>was</u> playing
           A

with the <u>computer,</u> but it
              B

<u>broke.</u> (<u>none</u>)
   C   D

☐ A   ☐ B   ☐ C   ☐ D

Variety / Lesson 29

cathy and me want to go to

---

juans family visited central zoo and they ate lunch at sauls deli

---

Ashley and <u>she</u> <u>have gone</u>
      A   B
to Adams Middle School to
<u>by</u> banners. (<u>none</u>)
 C   D

☐ A ☐ B ☐ C ☐ D

Variety / Lesson 30

he don't play at georges house

Her brothers tree growed twenty one inches last year

Mrs. Hunt <u>wanted</u> to read
         A
"<u>Summer</u>," a <u>poem</u> to her
   B   C
class. (<u>none</u>)
         D

☐ A   ☐ B   ☐ C   ☐ D

Paragraphs / Lesson 1

Thats when james realized he was in serious trouble. "I didn't mean to do it," james cried, "I was just teasing And playing games". "see me in my office", exclamed the principle.

Paragraphs / Lesson 2

Sweat glistened on his forehead. John was counting on this english test to bring up his grade point average. His science math social studies and health grades was all awfull; Therfore this test was his last chance.

Paragraphs / Lesson 3

Can young children learn to speak a foreighn lanuage. Yes they can. It is more easy to learn a language at a young age. After all children begin to learn there native language when they are babys. The best ages are to learn a new language is between seven and fourteen.

Paragraphs / Lesson 4

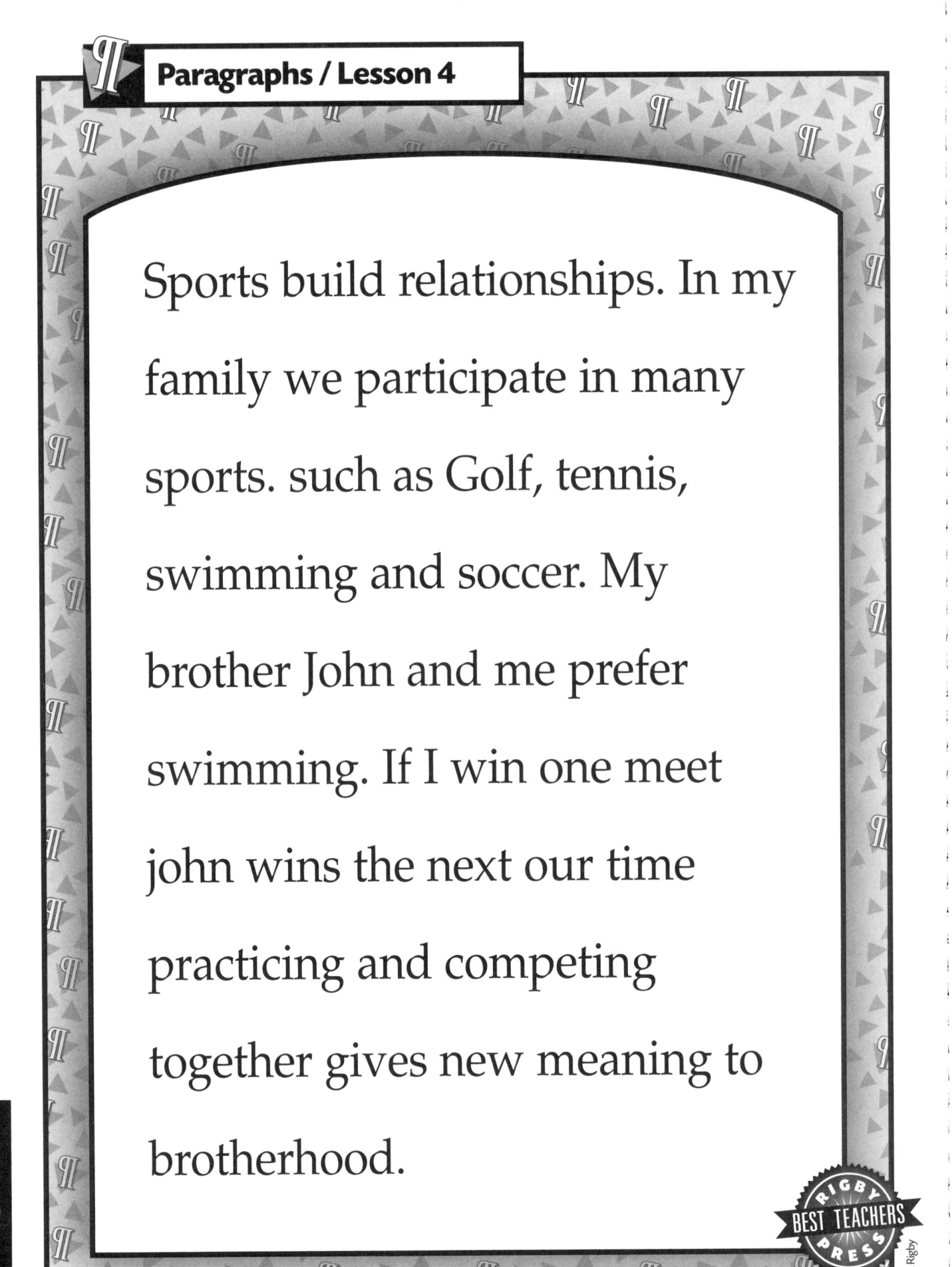

Sports build relationships. In my family we participate in many sports. such as Golf, tennis, swimming and soccer. My brother John and me prefer swimming. If I win one meet john wins the next our time practicing and competing together gives new meaning to brotherhood.

Paragraphs / Lesson 5

The alamo it still invokes pride in the citizens of texas. Many historical figures lost his life at the alamo as texas fought for it's independence from mexico. Today many americans and mexicans too visit the alamo.

Paragraphs / Lesson 6

Jane with a nervous hand wraped the heavy wool scarf around her neck. The cold morning air feeled the hallways of jefferson elementary school as the studnets darted toward class. "jane did you study for you're math test", asked Mrs. Smith? "No", said Jane.

Paragraphs / Lesson 7

The eating habits of rabbits has created the problems for gardeners throughout history. The constant crunching of carrots and other flora have infurriated the hard working gardener. To bring order man has developed ways to prevent rabbits from munching on the fruits of his labor.

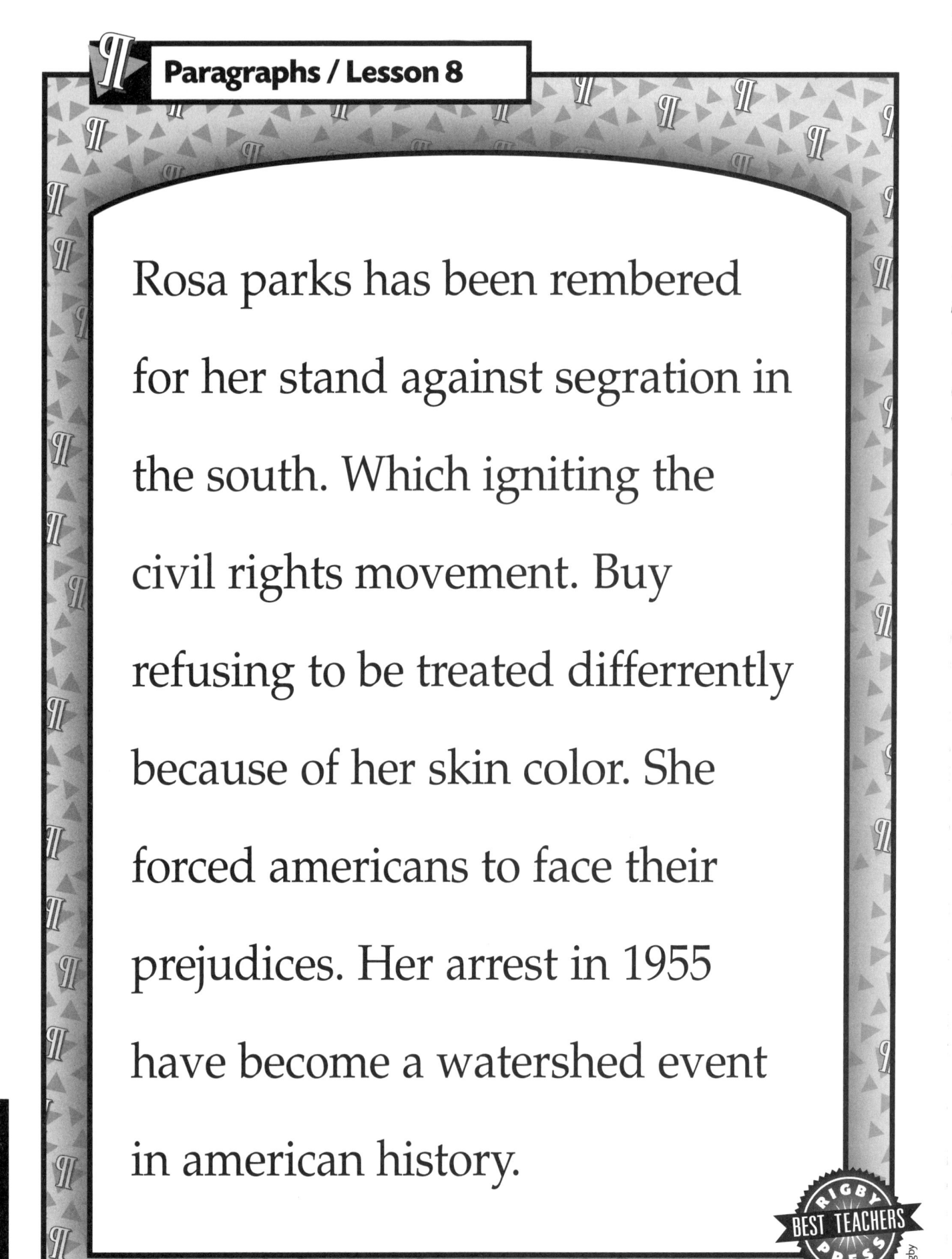

Rosa parks has been rembered for her stand against segration in the south. Which igniting the civil rights movement. Buy refusing to be treated differrently because of her skin color. She forced americans to face their prejudices. Her arrest in 1955 have become a watershed event in american history.

Paragraphs / Lesson 9

An artists work can inspire us. As we examine the color and the scene on a canvas we imagine ourselfs transported around the world or we can travel to other times such as the future and the past. You might one day inspire others if you hold the brush.

Paragraphs / Lesson 10

In the early ninteen hundreds the statue of liberty stood, her torch was held high, as she welcomed immigrants to her land. Many immigrants protestants, catholics and jews, was unskilled most spoke languages other than english. but they filled ellis island looking for a better life in the united states and have made our nation richer because of these different people.

Paragraphs / Lesson 11

Do you have a favorite book. I love pop up books. The anticipation of opening each page keeps me interested. John my best friend and me spend hours each saturday. Looking for pop up books at Sals corner book store.

Paragraphs / Lesson 12

Its time to turn off the television. Some children arent able to think create or play. They was consumed buy TV. When are we going to promote telivision free activities for children. The united states must encourige and support communitys to organize TV free activities.

Paragraphs / Lesson 13

Do you have a fear of being lost I do. When I was a young child my Mom read Hansel and Gretel to me and for a long time after it I was afraid of gettin lost or left. Since then I have wondered if it is wise to read these classic stories to kids to young to recognise them as fiction.

Paragraphs / Lesson 14

beneath the stately maple tree the sqirrel sit motinless. Suddenly it darts up the tree soundlessly and scamper out to the top most branch and I imagin what it feels like to run and jump and move about freely. My hands reach down to guide the wheels of my chair and I know I can only dream of moveing with out it.

Paragraphs / Lesson 15

"Jane my arm is caught", cried Brandon "As he tugged." "Give me you're other hand Brandon", urged Jane. The too of them was in trouble and they new it. Mom and dad had warned them to stay away from the swamp. Now it was to late.

Paragraphs / Lesson 16

The world had never looked so grim, martin and lukes only hope to make it to anchorage with out freezing was their sled that had crashed on the trail a few miles back. they knew there survival depended on moving forward. Without warning luke slumped down in to the snow. Martin cryed "Luke, don't give up. Be strong!

Paragraphs / Lesson 17

Sean stared at the broken down school bus and his lips quivered when he realized he would never be able to ride the bus again because Northside middle school didn't have no money to by another one. How was the children in the outlying areas going to get to scool.

Paragraphs / Lesson 18

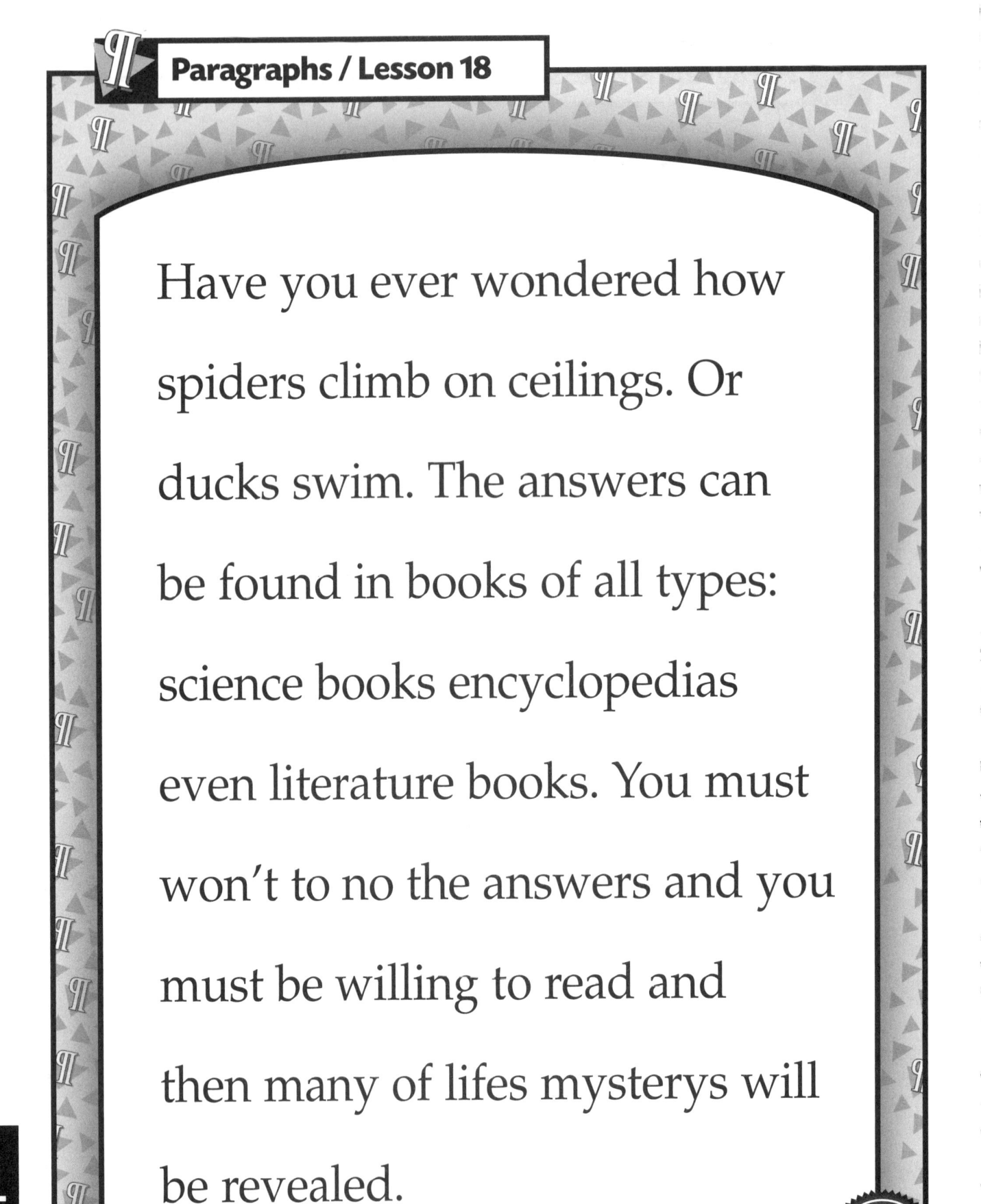

Have you ever wondered how spiders climb on ceilings. Or ducks swim. The answers can be found in books of all types: science books encyclopedias even literature books. You must won't to no the answers and you must be willing to read and then many of lifes mysterys will be revealed.

Paragraphs / Lesson 19

Glowing eyes flash in the headlights. It's hardened armor wraps tightly around the armadillo from amarillo as it darts among the cars. The texas mammal roams the countryside and highways even with it's ugly exterior it is loved by many native texans.

Paragraphs / Lesson 20

Today its the calander that rules our lives. Out of date events must be scratched off and new events must be added. Ball practice and choir practice have been scheduled today has that been changed to tuesday and when will we have a chance to watch the clouds and dream a dream. Its time to close the calendar and watch the couds.

Paragraphs / Lesson 21

The oversized picture book layed forlornly on the tabel. My fingers trembled as i moved them ever so slow toward the sinister looking book. My breathing quickened as my fingers was touching the cover moldy with age and neglect. My hare stood on end as the book let out a low growl.

Paragraphs / Lesson 22

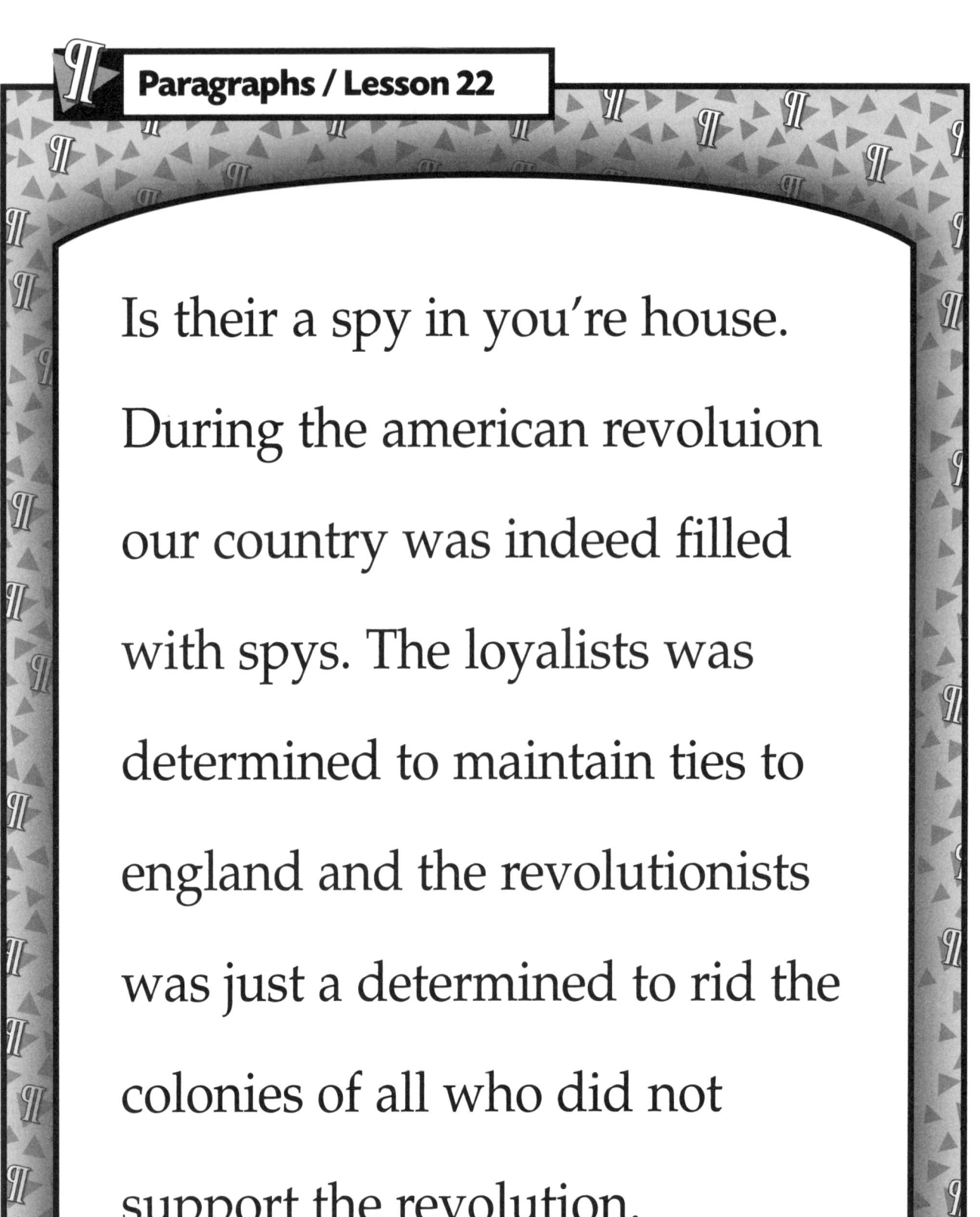

Is their a spy in you're house. During the american revoluion our country was indeed filled with spys. The loyalists was determined to maintain ties to england and the revolutionists was just a determined to rid the colonies of all who did not support the revolution.

Paragraphs / Lesson 23

Andrew and me quitely crouched behind the broken down car. Andrew don't know how to keep his giggles to himself. Hush i wispered don't you know you are going to get us caught. Behind us we herd movment. for a moment we both stopped breathing. I felt the hand on my shoulder a second befor I heard the raspy voice say what are you kids doing hear.

Paragraphs / Lesson 24

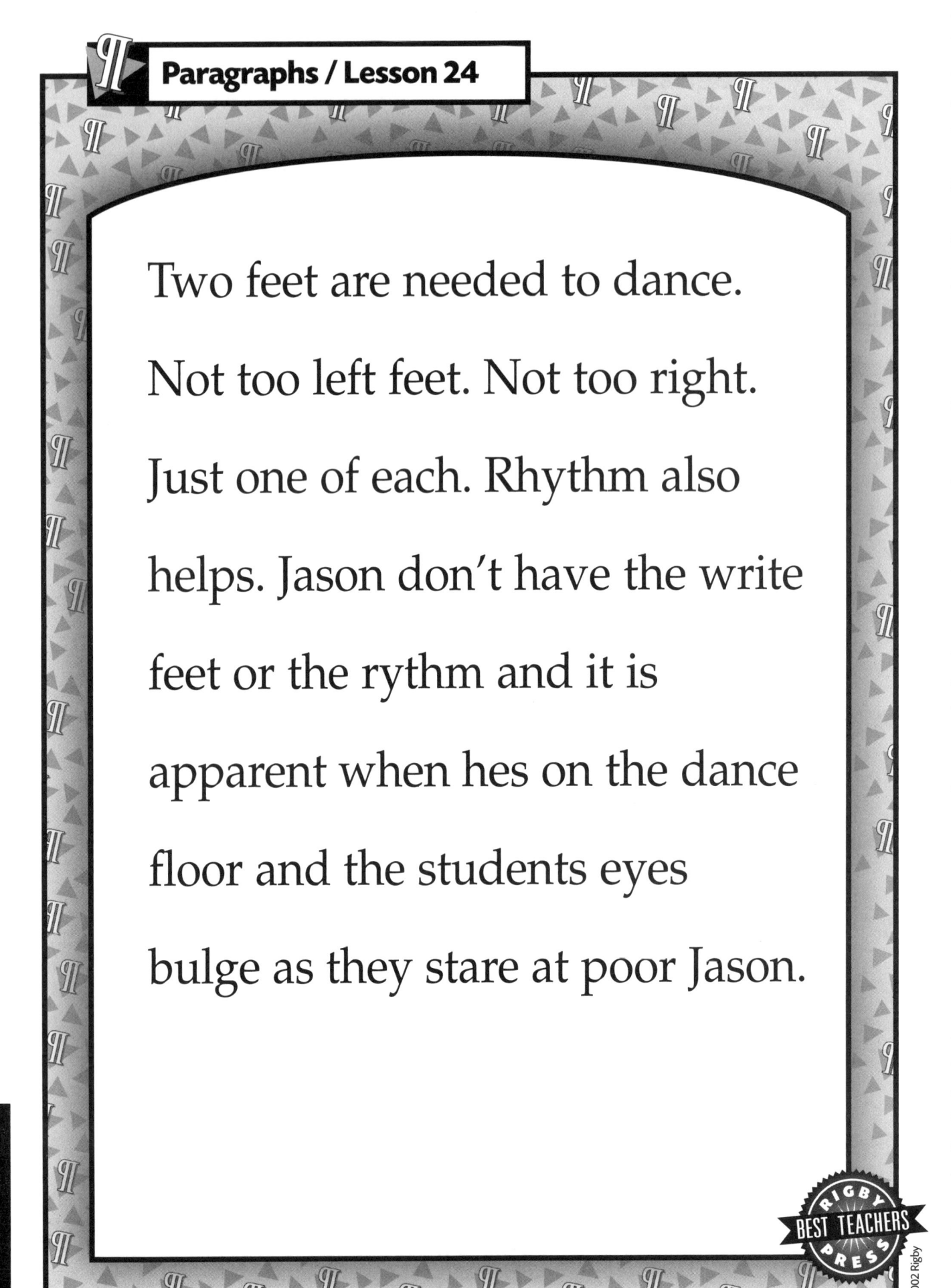

Two feet are needed to dance. Not too left feet. Not too right. Just one of each. Rhythm also helps. Jason don't have the write feet or the rythm and it is apparent when hes on the dance floor and the students eyes bulge as they stare at poor Jason.

Paragraphs / Lesson 25

Rhythmic sounds echo troughout the rain forest. Central america and south america are filled with the beauty of animals and plants living in natural harmony but people are destroying it all, we need to stop the mas destruction of are treasured forests. Do we wants to loose the sounds.

Paragraphs / Lesson 26

Is you're classroom feeled with books. If we won't to learn we must have books. easy to read books thin books science books and novels. wile the books themselves wont teach us how to read they provide us the tools for reading.

Dust can be a killer. The draught and dust storms of the 1930s destroyed the lifes of many. During the period historians refer too as the Dust bowl, 50 percent of the farmers in oklahoma went bankrupt and the starving people had to leave the state looking for work somewhere else and families went to california searching for a better life.

Paragraphs / Lesson 28

The world of bees is fascinating too many. Some scientists are so intrigued by bees that they study there wax production division of labor mating and death. indeed the social system of queen workers and drones can be a life long study for those truely interested.

Paragraphs / Lesson 29

The thought of a snake creeping on it's belly sends chills through a body. Their are 2,500 diffrent kinds of snakes in the world. They are found allmost everywhere on earth except the arctic antarctica iceland ireland and new zealand. They are present even when we are not aware of them. And although most are not harmful, there sudden appearence can be startling.

Paragraphs / Lesson 30

Is it a bird is it a plain no its an endangered bald eagle. In addition to bald eagles many other animals such as whooping cranes, grizzly bears and manatees are now on the endangered species list It is are responsibility to protect these animals and there environments. We must work hard to save these creatures as are world will be foerever changed without them.

Answer Key

✓ Usage

Usage / Lesson 1
Juan and I are going to the movies.
The children, screaming loudly, went out to play.
C me

Usage / Lesson 2
Devin ran every morning in the fall. (runs)
Greg and Meagan have been in two plays.
C knows

Usage / Lesson 3
Each student should complete her (his) test.
Everyone jumped on his (her) bike.
D (none)

Usage / Lesson 4
The teacher blamed us girls for everything.
Kyle is shorter than I.
B Janet and me

Usage / Lesson 5
Each student should open her (his) book.
Neither of the girls could find her ball.
C their

Usage / Lesson 6
The children drank their juice.
It was the warmest day of the year.
D (none)

Usage / Lesson 7
A group of sixth graders has been playing here. (had)
A herd of cows was sighted near the road. (is)
B nor

Usage / Lesson 8
In this story, the spelling and grammar are poor.
In the school, there are three sixth grade classes.
D (none)

Usage / Lesson 9
Ninety percent of the class is sick.
Matthew thought the guilty person was I.
— or —
Matthew thought I was the guilty person.
C I

Usage / Lesson 10
There are several reasons for checking his scores.
Everyone expected them to win the game.
D (none)

Usage / Lesson 11
They are smarter than we are.
If we were rich, we would purchase a new computer.
B we

Usage / Lesson 12
I cannot clean the table.
The new teacher doesn't like teaching her science class.
C all ready

Usage / Lesson 13
Paul is already late for class.
We cannot attend the rock concert.
A surely

Usage / Lesson 14
I didn't have time to do my homework.
— or —
I have no time to do my homework.
Joshua was lying on the sofa.
D (none)

Usage / Lesson 15
He set his book on the desk.
The Thanksgiving dinner tasted good.
— or —
The Thanskgiving dinner tasted very good.
D (none)

Ready, Set, Edit

Answer Key

Usage / Lesson 16
Moira is fixing the broken table.
A carton of eggs is on the table.
C is

Usage / Lesson 17
The boys are always arguing among themselves.
The class is winning the contest.
B are

Usage / Lesson 18
Either James or Kelly is to wash the dishes.
Paulo's sister received an A on the test.
B (omit "it") wins

Usage / Lesson 19
The suds are spilling on the floor.
Nobody in the class has finished the test.
D (none)

Usage / Lesson 20
Every student brought his (her) book.
The dog has its bone.
D (none)

Usage / Lesson 21
It was she who painted the picture.
If I were he, I would scream.
C him

Usage / Lesson 22
The teacher liked everyone but David and me.
When Alex saw the dog running down the street, he began to tremble.
C was

Usage / Lesson 23
Did David bring the book back yet?
Nick, I am sure, did run to his class.
B don't

Usage / Lesson 24
Jake decided to walk slowly and easily toward the house.
They played well in the tournament.
C (omit real) or really good

Usage / Lesson 25
We were late due to a power outage.
We practice for the play in the auditorium.
B because

Usage / Lesson 26
Where is the book?
Her face, sweaty and pale, was full of fear.
B (omit hardly)

Usage / Lesson 27
Tony fell off his bike.
Jackie blames Greg for the fight. (blamed)
D (none)

Usage / Lesson 28
She was angry with his dad.
I don't know if I passed the test.
D (none)

Usage / Lesson 29
Read that poem to John and me.
The skiers, Mary and she, plunged down the hill.
—or—
The skiers plunged down the hill.
D (none)

Usage / Lesson 30
The door's lock was broken.
He doesn't know the answer.
B quickly

Answer Key

Punctuation

Punctuation / Lesson 1
Michael, his father, is going to work.
He loaded his plate with chicken, fish, and bread.
C ?"

Punctuation / Lesson 2
Her long, wavy blond hair is beautiful.
Mark eats day-old bread, hot crispy pie, and homemade pizza.
B kind,

Punctuation / Lesson 3
Joe wants to play ball, but I want to read.
George wants to play ball and read.
A up (omit ,)

Punctuation / Lesson 4
It was a hot day, but Brandon loved it.
It's a lot of work, but the game is worth it.
B around (omit ,)

Punctuation / Lesson 5
Because I want a good grade, I will study hard.
I will study hard because I want a good grade.
B pool,

Punctuation / Lesson 6
Kevin, known as the class clown, ran out the door.
"How are you?" asked Marco.
C Brad,

Punctuation / Lesson 7
No, I do not want another book.
Sam, I think, is a wonderful student.
B town,

Punctuation / Lesson 8
Anyway, Dave agreed to dance.
Vinnie bought a shirt and then bought a jacket.
C and (omit ,)

Punctuation / Lesson 9
Juan, do you listen to WSTV?
Linda, that book is ours.
C PTA

Punctuation / Lesson 10
The students, James, John, and Vicki, failed the test.
Were there many 100s on the spelling test?
B twenty-five

Punctuation / Lesson 11
"You ate two-thirds of the cake!" exclaimed Jack.
Cheryl asked, "Have you read <u>Battle of the Giants</u> yet?"
B "Mary's Dance"

Punctuation / Lesson 12
Danny, an ex-teammate, shouted to his class.
The test completed, we began our math class.
A howling,

Punctuation / Lesson 13
The math test was very hard; therefore, many students did not pass.
Will you help me with my math, and then will you help me with my spelling?
C math (omit ,)

Punctuation / Lesson 14
Rebecca, we knew, was an excellent student.
Her class loved Mrs. Monroe, the well-known teacher.
D (none)

Punctuation / Lesson 15
If Jordan knew how to dance, he would be the hit of the party.
Greg would be the hit of the party if he knew how to dance.
B hard (omit ,)

Ready, Set, Edit

Answer Key

Punctuation / Lesson 16

Michael was born Wednesday, January 11, 1989, in Washington, Texas.

Thomas, John's best friend, moved to Littlefield, Texas last month.

B 2001,

Punctuation / Lesson 17

She likes to play two sports, basketball and soccer.

Do they have two pencils, three books, and one sheet of paper?

D (none)

Punctuation / Lesson 18

"The test is difficult; therefore, we should study," said Tom.

Emily said, "I will not study for the test; however, I will still pass."

A students

Punctuation / Lesson 19

Would you please open your book?

Sam asked, "Can you answer the question, Nick?"

C pie?"

Punctuation / Lesson 20

Mary treated her brothers the same—like babies.

"My friend who likes to dance went to John's class," said Sue.

B wallet (omit ,)

Punctuation / Lesson 21

You should read Poe's "The Raven." It is great.

"Should I write my report?" I wondered.

D (none)

Punctuation / Lesson 22

"I want," Omar remarked, "that old book."

"How are you?" Anna asked.

D (none)

Punctuation / Lesson 23

There are four 3s, seven rs, and five fourths in this problem.

Karen's friend was a freckle-faced boy.

B school (omit ,)

Punctuation / Lesson 24

Laney, a fifth grade student, wants to join the math club instead of the science club.

During the test, students became nervous.

D (none)

Punctuation / Lesson 25

John's class ate cherry pie, delicious cake, and hot muffins.

Dr. Horace's car, an old junk heap, is parked on the street.

D (none)

Punctuation / Lesson 26

No, I will not eat cake, cookies, or candy.

Todd's sister lives at 106 River Road, Shelby, New York.

B Thursday,

Punctuation / Lesson 27

Sara's dog stood at the corner; she would not move.

"Let's find its collar," said John.

B Scott,

Punctuation / Lesson 28

Mr. Smith, the teacher, liked to eat, write, and grade papers.

Having finished the test, Roger was ready to go to Sean's house.

A No,

Punctuation / Lesson 29

Tom's sister, I am sure, will cook chicken pie, bacon and eggs, and spiced apple cake for dinner.

It was a hot, humid July night, and I loved it.

C ?"

Answer Key

Punctuation / Lesson 30

"It's time to find Brian's dog," said Mark.

Jonas has lost his book; therefore, he must buy a new one.

B hard,

Aa Capitalization

Capitalization / Lesson 1

Steven and I will read the book.

The class will begin on Wednesday, May 3rd.

B principal

Capitalization / Lesson 2

Nicholas and Tonya could not find the English book.

Have you read The German Soldier?

A Smith

Capitalization / Lesson 3

Juan would like to play in the World Series for Boston.

Stuart and Katherine will perform in the play Pinballs.

C Spanish

Capitalization / Lesson 4

Even in the heat, I plan to run during May.

Andrew asked, "Do I have to play the flute?"

A Can

Capitalization / Lesson 5

President Lincoln lived in Washington during the Civil War.

Paul will study the Constitution for his history test.

B Thursday

Capitalization / Lesson 6

Have you read the poem, "The Walk Through the Woods"?

"Help me," called Tom, "my arm is broken!"

C history

Capitalization / Lesson 7

We will eat at Grandma Betty's house Thursday, Thanksgiving Day.

Jennifer Parker, president of Mode Company, will visit during Christmas vacation.

D (none)

Capitalization / Lesson 8

Mrs. Jackson smiled at you; oh, she is a great English teacher.

Neither Craig nor I plan to travel to North Carolina this fall.

C World Series

Capitalization / Lesson 9

"Don't leave the Norwegian cruise ship," warned Mark, "before it has dropped anchor."

Do you enjoy your Spanish, math, and English classes?

A Denver

Capitalization / Lesson 10

Tom and Joseph's poem was published in The News Times.

My favorite car is a Ford Taurus.

B English

Capitalization / Lesson 11

Mr. Kay moved to Texas from South Dakota last May.

They made a reservation at Hotel South, 108 New Street, Portland, Maine.

B cereal

Capitalization / Lesson 12

Miss Carson prefers Chicago to New York.

Mike asked, "Do you know the words to 'America the Beautiful'?"

B Mayor

Capitalization / Lesson 13

Julie and I were shopping at Beth's Boutique for a graduation dress.

Our street has become so busy we are moving to Elm Street.

A Saturday

Ready, Set, Edit 191

Answer Key

Capitalization / Lesson 14

I said, "I like to drink cola, lemonade, and root beer."

The Southside Wildcats will win the game Friday night.

D (none)

Capitalization / Lesson 15

After school, Mom asked me to finish my English homework.

Todd Fisher asked his mom to pick him up at Dyler Middle School.

A Mall

Capitalization / Lesson 16

I listened to Dr. Gold's speech on Friday.

On Monday Ken ate lunch at Southside Cafeteria.

B Thursday

Capitalization / Lesson 17

Colin could not find his American history book in the social studies classroom.

Elizabeth City is a pleasant city on the Pamlico River.

B Auditorium

Capitalization / Lesson 18

Jupiter and Mars can be viewed with a Thorson telescope.

Do you find calculus more difficult than English?

D (none)

Capitalization / Lesson 19

"Have you visited NASA in Florida?" asked Sue.

Greg and Steven read the poem "Sleeping in the Classroom" in English class.

D (none)

Capitalization / Lesson 20

The American eagle lives in the United States.

Matt named the Boston terrier Harry.

A Admiral

Capitalization / Lesson 21

I saw Mom talking to Senator Simms.

The class will plan a trip to the West next spring.

D (none)

Capitalization / Lesson 22

Carmen and I would like to join the Girl Scouts of America next fall.

The Spanish-speaking students enjoyed gelatin.

A March

Capitalization / Lesson 23

William enjoyed watching TV when he visited Canada and Mexico.

"Did Tom eat at the Italian restaurant?" asked Wayne.

C River

Capitalization / Lesson 24

The Orioles played in Denver, Colorado last Tuesday.

I'm sorry you broke the Roman vase.

B team

Capitalization / Lesson 25

My friend Admiral Hailey wanted to become a general.

I saw my mother and father shopping at Harvey Mall.

B team

Capitalization / Lesson 26

The Empire State Building will be closed for the Memorial Day holiday.

Is it broken, doctor?

B science

Capitalization / Lesson 27

Northside Middle School will prepare for President Bush's arrival.

Marta and I tutored the Russian students for their English test.

B buffalo

Answer Key

Capitalization / Lesson 28

Dr. Whitman earned his history degree from Duke University.

Mom, let's visit Yellowstone National Park next summer.

A America

Capitalization / Lesson 29

The manager's desk was covered with American Beauty roses.

Jake will visit South America and Canada next April.

C Mom

Capitalization / Lesson 30

Tom searched for Dr. Brown in the auditorium.

Tim said, "My English book is lost."

A Erie

Spelling

Spelling / Lesson 1

The girl had lovely brown hair.

Tom wants to go to his first class.

B answer

Spelling / Lesson 2

Brian accidentally stepped on the little creature.

The lightbulbs in the auditorium were brilliant.

D (none)

Spelling / Lesson 3

Chris wrote a poem for his assignment.

She likes arithmetic a lot.

C scary

Spelling / Lesson 4

Amy's cough created a rattle in her chest.

The assignment was due Wednesday.

C table

Spelling / Lesson 5

The class will usually find all the mistakes.

The students were sincerely sorry.

B quite

Spelling / Lesson 6

Rover growled at the people lined on the street.

He doesn't clean his room on Tuesday.

B trouble

Spelling / Lesson 7

They're having difficulty with arithmetic.

Several girls were excited about the February party.

A wouldn't

Spelling / Lesson 8

Sheila ate chocolate cake for dessert.

The doctor listened to the busy women.

A chose

Spelling / Lesson 9

Suzanne was amazed by the height of the building.

Sean was making his favorite chocolate cookies.

B straight

Spelling / Lesson 10

The teacher always wears pretty shoes.

The class was writing letters to friends.

A often

Spelling / Lesson 11

Tomorrow the students will practice for the game.

Bob enjoys traveling during summer vacation.

C first

Spelling / Lesson 12

Laura couldn't find Route 7 on the map.

Justin plays outside a lot on Saturday.

A doesn't

Ready, Set, Edit

Answer Key

Spelling / Lesson 13

The school bell will ring at any minute.

Neither boy would practice before the game.

C hospital

Spelling / Lesson 14

Charlie received a lovely gift from his aunt.

They were writing a book together.

B quarter

Spelling / Lesson 15

Rich wanted a third piece of cake.

The white shoes were left outside.

A Something

Spelling / Lesson 16

The new teacher will be forty years old tomorrow.

I thought the science lesson was easy.

B dairy

Spelling / Lesson 17

Russell went straight to the store to buy sugar for his mother.

The class built a playground for everyone.

A studying

Spelling / Lesson 18

Everyone was excited about the science experiment.

Did Michael embarrass the school principal?

A surprise

Spelling / Lesson 19

The class should not interrupt the principal.

Is fourth grade similar to fifth grade?

B pleasant

Spelling / Lesson 20

The boys looked at the new calendar.

Sue was the greatest athlete in sixth grade.

C restaurant

Spelling / Lesson 21

The students paid for the rhythm instruments.

Josh requested a receipt from the clerk.

A It's

Spelling / Lesson 22

The students tried to make all their poems rhyme.

Claire was a magnificent athlete.

A definition

Spelling / Lesson 23

The performance was inspirational.

The errors on the mathematics test were too numerous.

A niece

Spelling / Lesson 24

The students were probably dissatisfied.

The two friends were in separate classes.

C surprise

Spelling / Lesson 25

Patti is fascinated with mystery novels.

It never occurred to the friends to clean the aisle.

D (none)

Spelling / Lesson 26

Tim tried to be pleasant after the argument.

The new game was especially difficult.

B noticeable

Spelling / Lesson 27

It is not acceptable to interrupt the geography class.

The field trip was an incredible experience.

A arguing

Spelling / Lesson 28

The couple received their marriage license last Wednesday.

Tom gave a description of the cemetery to the teacher.

A transferred

Answer Key

Spelling / Lesson 29

We will probably proceed to the athletic field.

The muscles in his arm surprised Mel.

B exceeded

Spelling / Lesson 30

They don't appreciate my beneficial advice.

Steven examined the book thoroughly.

A vacuumed

Variety

Variety / Lesson 1

Sue Lamb popped the video into the VCR.

"Last night we watched a TV program about Mount Rushmore," said Henry.

B Washington

Variety / Lesson 2

Students have always needed to talk, eat, sleep, and play.

Now in order to play today, you must complete your work.

C quite

Variety / Lesson 3

While you're there, check out the English book.

After lunch, it's time to study the Constitution.

C House

Variety / Lesson 4

"If you know what you want," Luke says, "you will get it."

Soon his friends will start to laugh.

A Believing

Variety / Lesson 5

I want to be there to fix anything that goes wrong.

John really likes chatting on the telephone.

A Company

Variety / Lesson 6

President Clinton visited China.

Their best friends, Connie and Samantha, ate at Goldman's Restaurant.

A took (has taken)

Variety / Lesson 7

My friend and I don't like to visit the doctor.

Did you remind Kevin about Jennifer's birthday on Monday, April 7th?

A Yes,

Variety / Lesson 8

My mom plans to visit France next February.

"Set those boxes on the floor," said Tyler.

A will —or— B ever

Variety / Lesson 9

No, my dog won't play at Fairmont Park.

My brother and I took the books to school. (have taken)

B game

Variety / Lesson 10

"I hope Tonya's mom doesn't break anything," said Jimmy.

The school chorus sang "America the Beautiful."

A I

Variety / Lesson 11

Jane's mom bought a new book called <u>Time for Baking</u>.

The children didn't know it was President Washington's birthday.

A two

Variety / Lesson 12

Tell Mrs. Kimball, your new teacher, the school's schedule.

Her mom said, "Let's eat at Dave's Diner."

A doesn't

Answer Key

Variety / Lesson 13
Judy and I ate (have eaten) all the candy; therefore, we will have none left for the party.

"Put on your coat," said Mom, "and your gloves."

D (none)

Variety / Lesson 14
Have you seen Fido, my cat?

The two girls want to play at Kim's house.

B better

Variety / Lesson 15
Sam doesn't have transportation to Brookfield Park.

Did you thank Principal Johnson for the books, pencils, and computers?

A taught

Variety / Lesson 16
My dad threw a ball to Jordan and me.

Those books belong here on Miss Tyler's desk.

B West

Variety / Lesson 17
Did you find this book at the store?

Melissa and I shopped at Southside Department Store last Thursday.

A those (the)

Variety / Lesson 18
Ricardo and I didn't find any broken bikes at Joey's house.

Pete must sit quietly in Dr. Black's office.

D (none)

Variety / Lesson 19
The Howe family moved to Thirty-second Avenue, Charlotte, North Carolina, last July.

No, he doesn't belong here.

A gave (had given)

Variety / Lesson 20
Dear Mr. Perry,

Yours truly,

Jared Singleton

The Civil War was fought in the nineteenth century.

A I

Variety / Lesson 21
Greg and I would have gone there, but we were tired.

Sue and her mom celebrated at the restaurant on Pine Street.

C any

Variety / Lesson 22
Their class left on May 3, 2001, to go to Banter Park.

Jane and I ate all the cookies. (have eaten)

D (none)

Variety / Lesson 23
Paul is younger than his brother; therefore, he goes to a different school.

"Annie, you should have given your books to Juan," said Mom.

B went (have gone)

Variety / Lesson 24
Mom said, "Joe, these shoes don't fit your feet anymore."

Eduardo, you're planning, I know, to study hard for the test.

B were

Variety / Lesson 25
Tom and he ate (had eaten) before Mom arrived.

If you misbehave, you will not be allowed to visit East Park.

B School

Variety / Lesson 26

Maria read an excellent book about Australia written by Jake Venn.

"Tom, buy bread, milk, and sugar at East Market," said Dad.

C me

Variety / Lesson 27

Class, please sit quietly and listen to Mr. Garvey and me.

Mark studied his spelling, completed his math, and read the novel, The Tower of Terror.

D (none)

Variety / Lesson 28

Did you read the article called "Fire in the City" in last week's Times Magazine?

Ruth doesn't eat her vegetables, drink her milk, or clean her tray.

A were

Variety / Lesson 29

Cathy and I want to go, too.

Juan's family visited Central Zoo, and they ate lunch at Saul's Deli.

C buy

Variety / Lesson 30

He doesn't play at George's house.

Her brother's tree grew twenty-one inches last year.

C a poem,

Answer Key

¶ Paragraphs

> Keep in mind that the answers in this section represent one way that the paragraph could be corrected. Your students may think of other correct ways to fix the mistakes.

Paragraphs / Lesson 1

That's when James realized he was in serious trouble. "I didn't mean to do it," James cried, "I was just teasing and playing games."

"See me in my office!" exclaimed the principal.

Paragraphs / Lesson 2

Sweat glistened on his forehead. John was counting on this English test to bring up his grade point average. His science, math, social studies, and health grades were all awful; therefore, this test was his last chance.

Paragraphs / Lesson 3

Can young children learn to speak a foreign language? Yes, they can.

It is easier to learn a language at a young age. After all, children begin to learn their native language when they are babies. The best ages to learn a new language are between seven and fourteen.

Paragraphs / Lesson 4

Sports build relationships. In my family, we participate in many sports such as golf, tennis, swimming, and soccer. My brother John and I prefer swimming. If I win one meet, John wins the next. Our time practicing and competing together gives new meaning to brotherhood.

Paragraphs / Lesson 5

The Alamo still invokes pride in the citizens of Texas. Many historical figures lost their lives at the Alamo as Texas fought for its independence from Mexico. Today, many Americans and Mexicans visit the Alamo.

Paragraphs / Lesson 6

Answer Key

Jane, with a nervous hand, wrapped the heavy wool scarf around her neck. The cold morning air filled the hallways of Jefferson Elementary School as the students darted toward class. "Jane, did you study for your math test?" asked Mrs. Smith.

"No," said Jane.

Paragraphs / Lesson 7

The eating habits of rabbits have created problems for gardeners throughout history. The constant crunching of carrots and other flora has infuriated the hardworking gardener. To bring order, man has developed ways to prevent rabbits from munching on the fruits of his labor.

Paragraphs / Lesson 8

Rosa Parks has been remembered for her stand against segregation in the South, which ignited the civil rights movement. By refusing to be treated differently because of her skin color, she forced Americans to face their prejudices. Her arrest in 1955 has become a watershed event in American history.

Paragraphs / Lesson 9

An artist's work can inspire us. As we examine the color and the scene on a canvas, we imagine ourselves transported around the world or traveling to the future or the past. You might, one day, inspire others if you hold the brush.

Paragraphs / Lesson 10

In the early 1900s, the Statue of Liberty stood, her torch held high, as she welcomed immigrants to her land. Many immigrants—Protestants, Catholics, and Jews—were unskilled, and most spoke languages other than English. They filled Ellis Island looking for a better life in the United States and have made our nation richer.

Paragraphs / Lesson 11

Do you have a favorite book? I love pop-up books. The anticipation of opening each page keeps me interested. John, my best friend, and I spend hours each Saturday looking for pop-up books at Sal's Corner Bookstore.

Paragraphs / Lesson 12

It's time to turn off the television. Some children aren't able to think, create, or play. They are consumed by TV. When are we going to promote television-free activities for children? The United States must encourage and support communities that organize television-free activities.

Paragraphs / Lesson 13

Do you have a fear of being lost? I do. When I was a young child, my mom read Hansel and Gretel to me. For a long time after that, I was afraid of getting lost or being left behind. Since then I have wondered if it is wise to read these classic stories to children who are too young to recognize them as fiction.

Paragraphs / Lesson 14

Beneath the stately maple tree, the tiny squirrel sits motionless. Suddenly, he darts up the tree soundlessly and scampers out to the topmost branch. I imagine what it feels like to run and jump and move about freely. My hands reach down to guide the wheels of my chair. I know I can only dream of moving without it.

Paragraphs / Lesson 15

"Jane, my arm is caught," cried Brandon as he tugged.

"Give me your other hand, Brandon," urged Jane. The two of them were in trouble, and they knew it. Mom and Dad had warned them to stay away from the swamp. Now, it was too late.

Answer Key

Paragraphs / Lesson 16

The world had never looked so grim. Martin and Luke's only hope to make it to Anchorage without freezing was their sled that had crashed on the trail a few miles back. They knew their survival depended on moving forward. Without warning, Luke slumped down into the snow. Martin cried, "Luke, don't give up. Be strong!"

Paragraphs / Lesson 17

Sean stared at the broken-down school bus. His lips quivered when he realized he would never be able to ride the bus again. Northside Middle School had no money to buy another one. How were the children in the outlying areas going to get to school?

Paragraphs / Lesson 18

Have you ever wondered how spiders climb on ceilings or how ducks swim? The answers can be found in books of all types: science books, encyclopedias, even literature books. You must want to know the answers, and you must be willing to read. Then many of life's mysteries will be revealed.

Paragraphs / Lesson 19

Glowing eyes flash in the headlights. Hardened armor wraps tightly around the armadillo from Amarillo as it darts among the cars. The Texas mammal roams the countryside and highways. Even with its ugly exterior, it is loved by many native Texans.

Paragraphs / Lesson 20

Today, it's the calendar that rules our lives. Out-of-date events must be scratched off, and new events must be added. Ball practice and choir practice have been scheduled today. Has that been changed to Tuesday? When will we have a chance to watch the clouds and dream a dream? It's time to close the calendar and watch the clouds.

Paragraphs / Lesson 21

The oversized picture book lay forlornly on the table. My fingers trembled as I moved them ever so slowly toward the sinister-looking book. My breath quickened as my fingers touched the cover, moldy with age and neglect. My hair stood on end as the book let out a low growl.

Paragraphs / Lesson 22

Is there a spy in your house? During the American Revolution, our country was indeed filled with spies. The loyalists were determined to maintain ties to England, and the revolutionists were just as determined to rid the colonies of all whom did not support the revolution.

Paragraphs / Lesson 23

Andrew and I quietly crouched behind the broken-down car. Andrew didn't know how to keep his giggles to himself. "Hush," I whispered, "don't you know you are going to get us caught?" Behind us we heard movement. For a moment, we both stopped breathing.

I felt the hand on my shoulder a second before I heard the raspy voice say, "What are you kids doing here?"

Paragraphs / Lesson 24

Two feet are needed to dance, not two left feet or two right—just one of each. Rhythm also helps. Jason doesn't have the right feet or the rhythm, and it is apparent when he's on the dance floor. The students' eyes bulge as they stare at poor Jason.

Paragraphs / Lesson 25

Rhythmic sounds echo throughout the rainforest. Central America and South America are filled with the beauty of animals and plants living in natural harmony, but people are destroying it all. We need to stop the mass destruction of our treasured forests. Do we want to lose the sounds?

Answer Key

Paragraphs / Lesson 26
Is your classroom filled with books? If we want to learn, we must have books—easy to read books, thin books, science books, and novels. While the books themselves won't teach us to read, they provide the tools for reading.

Paragraphs / Lesson 27
Dust can be a killer. The drought and dust storms of the 1930s destroyed the lives of many. During the period historians refer to as the Dust Bowl, fifty percent of the farmers in Oklahoma went bankrupt. The starving people had to leave the state looking for work somewhere else. Families went to California searching for a better life.

Paragraphs / Lesson 28
The world of bees is fascinating to many. Some scientists are so intrigued by bees that they study their wax production, division of labor, mating habits, and death. Indeed, the social system of queen, workers, and drones can be a lifelong study for those truly interested.

Paragraphs / Lesson 29
The thought of a snake creeping on its belly sends chills through a body. There are 2,500 different kinds of snakes in the world. They are found almost everywhere on Earth except the Arctic, Antarctica, Iceland, Ireland, and New Zealand. They are present even when we are not aware of them, and although most are not harmful, their sudden appearance can be startling.

Paragraphs / Lesson 30
Is it a bird? Is it a plane? No, it's an endangered bald eagle. In addition to bald eagles, many other animals such as whooping cranes, grizzly bears, and manatees are now on the endangered species list. It is our responsibility to protect these animals and their environments. We must work hard to save these creatures as our world will be forever changed without them.